D0871658

'Talk not about who does well or badly; seek where you yourself fall short.'

(HOZOIN SCHOOL, 1600 A.D.)

Judo Memoirs of Jigoro Kano

EARLY HISTORY OF JUDO

Brian N. Watson

AMHERST PUBLIC LIBRARY
221 SPRING STREET
AMHERST, OHIO 44001

Trafford
PUBLISHING

Order this book online at www.trafford.com/07-2910
or email orders@trafford.com

Most Trafford titles are also available at major online book retailers.

© Copyright 2008 Brian N. Watson.

All rights reserved. No part of this publication may be reproduced, stored in a retrieval
system, or transmitted, in any form or by any means, electronic, mechanical, photocopying,
recording, or otherwise, without the written prior permission of the author.

Note for Librarians: A cataloguing record for this book is available from Library
and Archives Canada at www.collectionscanada.ca/amicus/index-e.html

ISBN: 978-1-4251-6349-5

*We at Trafford believe that it is the responsibility of us all, as both individuals
and corporations, to make choices that are environmentally and socially sound.
You, in turn, are supporting this responsible conduct each time you purchase a
Trafford book, or make use of our publishing services. To find out how you are
helping, please visit www.trafford.com/responsiblepublishing.html*

*Our mission is to efficiently provide the world's finest, most comprehensive
book publishing service, enabling every author to experience success.
To find out how to publish your book, your way, and have it available
worldwide, visit us online at www.trafford.com/10510*

 www.trafford.com

North America & international
toll-free: 1 888 232 4444 (USA & Canada)
phone: 250 383 6864 ✦ fax: 250 383 6804 ✦ email: info@trafford.com

The United Kingdom & Europe
phone: +44 (0)1865 487 395   local rate: 0845 230 9601
facsimile: +44 (0)1865 481 507   mail: info.uk@trafford.com

10 9 8 7

Professor Jigoro Kano

'The purpose of judo is to perfect oneself
physically, intellectually and morally
for the benefit of society.'

PROFESSOR JIGORO KANO (1860-1938)

FOUNDER OF JUDO

DEDICATION

This book is dedicated to the memory of Trevor Pryce Leggett and to Donn F. Draeger both of whom attempted to achieve the judo ideal and by example inspired others.

Japanese Personal Names

The Japanese custom is to put the family name first and then the given name, such as Kano Jigoro. Throughout this book, however, the English custom has been observed for all Japanese personal names.

Author's Note

Most of the material contained in this book relates to the experiences of Jigoro Kano in his founding of judo. It is his verbal recollection of historical events, especially those that occurred from 1882 to 1928. Occasionally, there is some repetition of content by Kano. In the interests of both relevance and clarity it was at times deemed necessary to include it, although this has been avoided wherever possible.

Acknowledgements

I wish to express sincerest appreciation to those who graciously gave assistance in the preparation of the manuscript. For furnishing photographs, my thanks are due to Yukimitsu Kano, President of the Kodokan International Judo Center, Tokyo, and to Yoshinobu Yoshino of the Nippon Budokan, Tokyo. I am also indebted to Naoki Murata; Keith L. Hager; Associate Professor Kosuke Nagaki of Hyogo Kyouiku University; Professor Shuichi Okada, Kobe University; Professor Shunsuke Yamasaki, Konan University; Associate Professor Shinya Sogabe, Konan University; Professor Masaru Yano, Wakayama University; Lecturer Takuto Ikeda, Wakayama University; and to Associate Professor Hiroki Furusumi, University of Hyogo, for their kind assistance in reviewing the translated proofs prior to publication.

CONTENTS

PREFACE

Jigoro Kano is known among enthusiasts of martial arts worldwide as the creator of judo. In Japan, however, he is also known for inspiring the Japanese Olympic team following defeat in its first three appearances at the games of 1912, 1920 and 1924, to gold medal successes that were achieved in 1928 at the Amsterdam Olympics, and which still continue today. But more notably, he is known for his work in helping to introduce reforms to Japan's system of education. Kano, perhaps more than any other Japanese educator of his generation, encouraged a host of Tokyo Teacher Training College students to become dedicated to the teaching profession and to the promotion of sporting education. Because of his positive commitment to the furtherance of physical education, to judo and to teacher training, the resulting physical development and scholastic attainment of Japanese children, particularly those receiving compulsory education, was greatly influenced by Kano in the 1900s and in the decades thereafter. Thus, the fruits of his endeavors contributed in some measure to the improvement in health and in the enhanced skills of many of the nation's workforce that manifested itself in the subsequent robust expansion of Japan's economy.

Unfortunately for those with a keen interest in the history of judo, Jigoro Kano did not write his autobiography. Therefore, although others, both individuals and groups of scholars, have written biographies on Kano, little detailed information actually penned by the man himself, especially concerning his family life and the development of his dojo 'Kodokan', has been available for publication. Nonetheless, in a string of interviews that he gave in his mid-sixties, he did recount to his interviewer, Torahei Ochiai, a high school principal and former student of Kano, many of his experiences. Kano's dictations surrounding the early history of judo were compiled and preserved in print by

Ochiai. These first appeared as a series of magazine articles in the late 1920s. This material also included incidents from Kano's school days, his training in jujutsu, together with his experiences in academia, overseas travels, and some aspects of his private life. Perhaps most significantly though, particularly for the followers of judo, he related much information on his establishment, promotion and later extensive expansion of the Kodokan, which became for him an obsessive, life-long commitment.

In 1877, Kano began learning Tenjin Shinyo jujutsu, initially under the regular tutelage of Hachinosuke Fukuda. Two years later Fukuda died. Following the passing of his second Tenjin Shinyo jujutsu master, Masatomo Iso, he took up the study of Kito style jujutsu with Tsunetoshi Iikubo. In May 1882, while still an unknown university student of twenty-one, he opened his small, nondescript Kodokan dojo in downtown Tokyo, where he taught jujutsu to his first class of nine students. His choice of the name 'Kodokan' symbolizes precocity in one so young and is highly significant, for it means 'the institute where one is guided along the road to follow in life', that is to say, a road that one travels as a means of self-cultivation, which Kano regarded as the optimum way to live one's life. This cultivation of the spirit, however, can only be attained following long years of training that is made with vigorous exertion in an effort to reach the ultimate goal: self-perfection.

At the age of twenty-four, shortly after qualifying as a master of Kito style jujutsu, Kano abruptly gave up the teaching of this ancient and altogether brutal activity and never taught jujutsu again. In his attempt to create for the modern age a non-violent, spiritually inspiring antagonistic art, he carried out research on several other styles of jujutsu. Primarily in the interests of both safety and practicality, he altered and added his own devices to many of the techniques that he was later to incorporate into his newly conceived system of skills, which he named officially as 'Kodokan judo'. In his subsequent lectures on judo, Kano often stated the following: 'The ultimate object of studying judo is to train and cultivate body and mind through practice in attack and defense, and by thus mastering the essentials of the art, to attain perfection of oneself and bring benefits to the world.' He had sought to create in judo, therefore, something positive out of something largely negative. He nurtured his art of judo, promoted it nationwide and later globally to young and old, male and female, for the remainder of his days.

Kano was a man of many parts. At the young age of twenty-five, he was appointed professor of political science and economics at both Komaba

Agricultural School and at the peers' school, Gakushuin. He afterward became head of the Tokyo Teachers' Training College, a post that he held for over twenty years. Kano was also a prolific essayist, translator, calligrapher, editor, sports administrator and towards the end of his life, a politician. Of all his varied interests though, the elevation of Japan's educational standards, the furtherance of Kodokan judo and the advancement of moral education were perhaps his most important considerations throughout life. Kano's ideals are borne out in the messages expressed in his essays and in his calligraphy, for often they emphasize the crucial importance of sound education, the fostering of a determined spirit as well as endeavoring to help improve the well-being of humankind. In a 1934 speech, he was quoted as saying: 'Nothing under the sun is greater than education. By educating one person and sending him into the society of his generation, we make a contribution extending to a hundred generations to come.' This message is conveyed and preserved in one of the most famous examples of his calligraphy.

Judging from some of his comments in the pages that follow, it would seem that it was mainly because of his earnest desire to advance education in Japan that he created judo; for he believed that the experiences derived from judo training can have a positive impact on both the general health as well as on the character development of students. In the case of traditional jujutsu though, Kano had realized quite early in life that it had drawbacks and was therefore an unsuitable activity for civilized society in the modern age. In particular, being purely a ruthless means of self-preservation, there are few rules observed in practice, and as he saw it, few positive benefits that would help lead to the all-round wholesome development of the student's character. Practice sessions are in essence combat, and therefore there is always an element of danger, especially so when edged weapons are employed. On the other hand, judo, in which no weapons are used, eventually became regulated as a sport, and as such is practiced in relative safety not only by able-bodied men, women and children but even by many of those who are in some way physically challenged.

Kano devoted much time and energy throughout life to educational research. He made thirteen official overseas voyages in order to report on the systems of education then current in foreign countries, particularly physical education in the West. On those occasions, he also attempted to generate international interest in Kodokan judo by means of his many demonstrations, lectures, and media interviews that he gave during his worldwide travels.

By being both a member of the International Olympic Committee for over twenty years and one of the founders and the first chairman of the Japan Amateur Sports Association, Kano was instrumental in helping to boost the popularity of Olympic sports, especially so among young Japanese.

Some of his comments in the pages that follow suggest that whatever worthwhile goals one wishes to achieve in life, first and foremost one must endeavor to preserve one's health, develop both a robust physique and a spirit of perseverance prior to the pursuit of one's objectives, for without these basic prerequisites, one can accomplish little of genuine substance. Perseverance, he maintained, can be inculcated in a trainee and further enhanced as a result of dedicated and disciplined judo training. In creating judo, therefore, he had attempted to devise a means of instilling intense motivation in his students. He advised them all, no matter what major field of study they were engaged in, to undertake such training, for besides helping to keep them fit, he believed that their will to succeed in life would also be increasingly strengthened.

The prime objectives in writing this book are twofold: to consider to what extent Kano's aims, especially with regard to judo, have been achieved, and to consider the impact that these aims have had on society. In the concluding part of this work, I have therefore commented on some of the effects that judo has had and continues to have on Japanese society, together with some of the experiences and accomplishments of three individuals in particular, both Japanese and non-Japanese, who were inspired by Kano's teachings. In describing the attainments of such men, however, I purposely did not choose to focus on any of the world's leading judo champions, either past or present, for the vast majority of those who train in judo are the non-competitive players, and as such seldom receive any kind of public recognition. And of course, we should not forget that Kano was insistent on judo being practiced primarily in order for it to be of some benefit to one in life. In fact it was Kano's contention that judo is a means for fostering development of both body and mind and he was, therefore, strongly against the conversion of judo into a sport. Judo, he maintained, is one of the budo arts and as such it is a means for cultivating courage, virtue and the intellect, all of which have crucial bearing on one's contentment in life. He did not wish to see judo become an imitation of other sports, where the sole objective of most practitioners is realized merely in the winning of medals. He made the following comments in this regard in a letter to Gunji Koizumi in 1936: 'I have been asked by people of various sections as to the wisdom and the possibility of judo being introduced at the Olympic

Games. My view on the matter, at present, is rather passive. If it be the desire of other member countries, I have no objection. But I do not feel inclined to take any initiative. For one thing, judo in reality is not a mere sport or game. I regard it as a principle of life, art and science. In fact, it is a means for personal cultural attainment. Only one of the forms of judo training, the so-called *randori* can be classed as a form of sport. In addition, the Olympic Games are so strongly flavored with nationalism that it is possible to be influenced by it and to develop Contest Judo as a retrograde form, as jujitsu was before the Kodokan was founded. Judo should be as free as art and science from external influences – political, national, racial, and financial or any other organized interest. And all things connected with it should be directed to its ultimate object, the benefit of humanity.'

Kano's ideals were, therefore, quite profound and thought provoking. Although judo has been a relatively popular participant sport in many countries around the world for decades, I have, nevertheless, concentrated most of my comments on Kano, his teachings, and in particular the effects that judo has had on Japanese society. This is because the history of judo in other societies is much briefer and thus its effect has been much less pronounced than that of Japan. These matters are further referred to in the concluding part of this book.

Some people seem capable of dealing effectively with many of their personal problems in life, and as a result they often gain in self-confidence. Others, however, facing similar difficulties are unable to overcome them and sometimes suffer. Occasionally this leads to sad consequences of self-harm; for some seek escape from their troubles in drink, in reckless gambling or perhaps increasingly in this day and age in the over dependency or misuse of drugs. In such instances though, rarely do their problems disappear, for on the contrary, they often multiply, causing them further physical pain or mental anguish. Is there something that one can derive from judo training that can possibly help one when tackling such problems? Judging from Kano's observations in the pages that follow, he seemed to think so, for he believed that once a spirit of determination has been acquired; it can be focused to challenge with tenacity any other difficulty that one may seek to overcome in life.

Kano seems to have been a popular figure in his day, for his academic students together with his judo trainees numbered in the tens of thousands. This was, of course, long before the days of instant fame often afforded to modern-age media personalities. Although his charisma gained for him a considerable following; we have to bear in mind the question: Do his teachings have any relevance today? After reading through the following pages, some may perhaps agree with his opinions and his aspirations in regard to sport, judo and education while no doubt others will disagree. Nonetheless, on this occasion consideration of divergent opinions does not fall within my purview for I merely wish to explain, as accurately as I can, his methods and the objectives that he tried so hard to attain, not necessarily to take sides on any specific issue. Naturally, in such a study one must always try to keep a sense of balance. One could reasonably argue, for instance, that there are judo enthusiasts who have been champions in youth, but later have failed to accomplish a similar level of success in other avenues of life. Then again, there are those youths who have had no experience of judo or indeed sport of any kind but who have nevertheless benefited in some way from experiences of a different kind and who have made a success of their lives.

In 2000, I published *The Father of Judo* (Kodansha International) a biography of Jigoro Kano, directed at young readers, which gives an overview of some personal details of his life. This present study, however, rather than private affairs, concentrates more on both the difficulties he encountered and the efforts he made in trying to further the aims of the Kodokan. Many of Kano's comments on these and other relevant matters are to be found in the succeeding part of this book, which contains my English rendition of Torahei Ochiai's above-mentioned Japanese-language reports that first appeared in print as a series of articles issued from January 1927 to December 1928 in the monthly Kodokan Culture Council magazine *Sako*.

In 1992 all of the above discourse by Kano, together with a number of his essay contributions to the monthlies *Judo* and *Yuko no Katsudo,* were collated and re-published in *Kano Jigoro Chosakushu* (Collected Works of Jigoro Kano) volume III.

Brian N. Watson

JUDO MEMOIRS OF JIGORO KANO

TRANSLATED BY BRIAN N. WATSON

1. Establishment of the Kodokan

People often ask me why I took up the study of jujutsu and why I founded the Kodokan. The motivation that I had for beginning the study of jujutsu is completely different from that which I relate today when explaining my reasons for creating judo. As a small boy, naturally, I studied many subjects, classical Chinese, calligraphy, English, and so on. Later, in 1873, I left home for the first time to enter a boarding school, Ikuei Gijuku, located in Karasumori-cho, Shiba, Tokyo.

Even though the headmaster at Ikuei Gijuku was Dutch and his assistant German, all subjects were taught in the English language. Before entering this boarding school, I had learned to read elementary English at a private school run by Shuhei Mizukuri. Therefore, at Ikuei Gijuku I was equal to my classmates in English ability. Among my fellow pupils there were some who were physically weak and as a result they were often under the domination of the bigger, stronger boys. The weaker ones were forced to serve the stronger. Since I was one of the weakest, I was made to run errands at the behest of the strong. Even at my age today, I am still physically as robust as the next man. However, in those days, although not sickly, I was, nevertheless, quite feeble. In general scholarly pursuits I was on a par with my classmates, but even so I was often treated by them with contempt and despised. From an early age my curiosity had been aroused when I first heard mention of jujutsu, a method of fighting whereby one with little strength, can overcome a physically more powerful adversary. I therefore seriously considered taking up training in this art.

At that time, a former soldier named Nakai frequented our house. He sometimes bragged that he knew jujutsu and showed me some *kata* techniques; this experience fired both my interest and imagination and gave me the idea of learning it from him. When I then asked him to teach me, however, he refused, saying that it was not necessary to learn jujutsu nowadays.

In addition to our family home in Mikage, my father owned a second house in Maruyama-cho, Koishikawa-ku, Tokyo. The caretaker of this house was Ryuji Katagiri. He occasionally showed me some jujutsu. I once asked him to give me regular instruction, but he also declined my request, saying that there was no point in learning it, since it was no longer of any practical use. Another frequent visitor to our house was Genshiro Imai of Higo in Kyushu, who had learned the Kyushin style of jujutsu. When I asked him to coach me, yet again I was refused. In fact, I could not find anyone who was willing to instruct me. As a result, I continued to suffer at the hands of bullies. Later, my school, Ikuei Gijuku, was moved to the site of the Okuma Hall and in 1874 I transferred to the English Language Department of the Tokyo School of Foreign Languages where the present Commercial College is located. Among my fellow students taking the entrance examination with me was the late Takaaki Kato, a former prime minister, and Dr. Kumazo Tsuboi who also studied at the same university as I until our graduation. After a time, the English Language Department at this school was hived off and a separate state-run English Language School was established. I attended this English Language School. While studying there, arrangements were made for me to lodge at the house of the principal of the Tokyo School of Foreign Languages, Shosaku Hida, since he was a friend of my father. Unlike Ikuei Gijuku, I was not bullied much at my new school chiefly because the classes were much smaller. However, after a time, I again realized that I needed to become stronger physically.

In 1875, I entered Kaisei School. Although scholastic ability was esteemed among the boys at Kaisei, I soon came to realize that physical prowess was in fact respected there even more than at Ikuei Gijuku. I still kept up with my classmates in scholastic attainments, but as for my physical abilities, I was nowhere nearly as strong or as robust as they were. Thus the urge in me to learn jujutsu finally became overwhelming. At last I approached my father and requested that he ask his colleagues, who had knowledge of jujutsu, to teach me. He disagreed with my decision, however, saying that there was no need for me to learn it. I soon came to realize that I could not rely on my father for any help in this quest. I was seventeen at that time and made up my mind that I had better learn to do things for myself, so I determined to find a jujutsu master by my own efforts.

I entered the Literature Department of Tokyo Imperial University in 1877. As I recall it was about that time that I hit upon the idea of enquiring at bonesetters' clinics, since it was said that many bonesetters had been jujutsu masters earlier in life, though I soon discovered that most of them had no knowledge of jujutsu. Other bonesetters whom I asked said that they used to teach jujutsu, but gave up the practice years ago. One day, I happened to be in Ningyocho, Nihonbashi, near the famous Benkei Bridge when I spotted an osteopath's signboard. I approached the doorway. The name on the signboard read, 'Teinosuke Yagi, Bonesetter'. Inside the building, I met a white-haired man who, despite advancing years, appeared to be strong and sturdy. I asked him if he gave instruction in jujutsu. He stared at me and wished to know why I asked such a question. I told him who I was and that I longed to learn jujutsu. He looked surprised at first and then smiled. He said that he was pleased to hear that I had an interest in the art and informed me that he had been awarded a license to teach jujutsu from Master Mataemon Iso. He said that years ago he had been very active in teaching, but had given up jujutsu and these days relied solely on bonesetting for his livelihood. He remarked that his eight-mat room was the only property he owned and that it was far too small for use as a jujutsu dojo. After some thought, he said that his other fellow instructors had quit teaching a long time back but that nearby, in what used to be Daiku-cho, there lived a jujutsu colleague of his, Master Hachinosuke Fukuda. Yagi then offered to introduce me and suggested that I go to Mr. Fukuda's dojo.

I left Yagi's clinic and went directly to the Fukuda dojo. It consisted of a ten-mat room with a stairway in one corner; the practice area was thus reduced to nine mats. There was an adjacent room of three mats where Fukuda treated his patients. Consequently, the nine-mat dojo was also used as a waiting room for Fukuda's patients. It was there; in that cramped dojo that I began my longed-for pursuit of the ancient secrets of jujutsu. The style taught there was Tenjin Shinyo that had been created by Master Mataemon Iso who had combined two of the older styles, the Yoshin and the Shin no Shinto. When I joined the dojo, Fukuda had but five students. Of these, only two trained regularly: one student practiced everyday, the other every two days.

Fukuda was formerly an instructor in jujutsu at the Kobusho, the government-run military training center where many of the offspring of samurai were trained in the full gamut of traditional martial arts. In addition, trainees received instruction in the use of cannon and small arms. His position there was equal to that of a university assistant professor. At the Kobusho, several styles of jujutsu were taught; among them were the Kito style and the Yoshin style. Occasionally, contests were held between those trained in Tenjin Shinyo and those trained in other styles. The most popular style in those days was the Yoshin. Master Hikosuke Totsuka was employed there and he had a large contingent of well-trained young men. Although Fukuda was an expert, in practice sessions against the Yoshin style of the Totsuka men I heard that he was very hard pressed.

The two men that I trained with most frequently in my early days at the Fukuda dojo were a Mr. Aoki and a local fish wholesaler, Kanekichi Fukushima, although Fukushima weighed some 90 kilograms, was physically strong and skillful, he knew very little about the theoretical side of jujutsu or *kata*. I learned *kata* daily from Fukuda. I did physical training exercises and often practiced *randori* with Aoki. Sometimes though, when Aoki was absent and Fukuda was injured, I had no partner. At that time, Fukuda made me practice break falls on my own. On some occasions, I had no training partner for several days in a row. Nevertheless, I still went to the dojo daily and did much physical exercise.

2. Pain is a Good Teacher

In those days, teaching methods were quite different from today. One method that I recall in particular was the day when Fukuda threw me down repeatedly. I immediately picked myself up the first time and asked him to explain how he did the throw. He merely said, "Attack again", which I did, and he threw me down once more. I faced him and repeated my question. Fukuda would only say; "Come on!" and yet again I was thrown. He then shouted, "Do you think you will learn jujutsu by mere explanations each time? Attack again". Once more I was thrown to the mat. By this method, he taught me how to do the throw by my experiencing the sensation of being pulled off balance and thrown by that particular technique. As I recall, the throw I learned very quickly that day was *sumi-gaeshi*.

When I took up jujutsu, there was little advice given to trainees so that they might avoid suffering the many minor aches and pains resulting from the rough and tumble of every day training sessions. We tended to practice techniques in a vigorous manner; using our muscles in bodily positions and in situations that are very rarely experienced in normal every day life. Thus, quite often the following morning the joints in my whole body ached so much that I sometimes had great difficulty in getting out of bed, let alone standing up and walking. Despite such discomfort though, I continued to train daily and never took a day off. Often I would limp to the dojo. Another thing that made training such a painful experience was the training wear, which was very different from that worn today. The trousers were little more than shorts, reaching only half way down the thigh and the jackets had very short, loose fitting sleeves reaching midway down the biceps. Therefore, our exposed elbows, knees and shins were often bruised or grazed during practice sessions. On my injured limbs I would sometimes smear a poultice, the brand name of which was Mankinko. Because the stench of this ointment was so overpowering, my dormitory roommates often complained and taunted me. Even today when I meet them, they still remind me and ridicule me about my use of Mankinko.

As I mentioned earlier, there were few trainees practicing regularly at Fukuda's dojo at that time. Since I was extremely keen to learn jujutsu, I desperately needed more training partners. I therefore made earnest efforts to recruit some of my fellow university students and asked them to accompany me to the dojo with a view to persuading them to take up the practice of jujutsu. Unfortunately, most of them soon quit. My best friend, Ryusaku Godai, however, continued with training for a time, but later he had to leave Tokyo and move to Yokosuka in order to complete his studies for his doctorate in engineering. He therefore gave up jujutsu training entirely. This was a big disappointment for me. Had he continued to train, I have no doubt that he would have become an expert in martial arts.

Perhaps the most memorable event of my days at the Fukuda dojo occurred in 1879 when U.S. President Ulysses Simpson Grant visited Japan on his world tour. The noted industrialist and philanthropist Eiichi Shibusawa, who later became an associate of mine, wished to entertain the president and his entourage with a demonstration of jujutsu. Shibusawa contacted Masatomo Iso and other jujutsu masters and invited them to his summer residence in

Asuyama in order to stage a display in honor of the president's visit. Godai and I were called upon to give an exhibition of *randori*. The well-known U.S. columnist, Julian Street, wrote an account of our demonstration which later appeared in the press.

In August 1879, shortly after this event, Master Fukuda collapsed and died. At that time, there were a number of other trainees at the dojo who were more skilled in *randori* than I. However, since I was the only one who regularly attended the training sessions and thus had a fair knowledge of both *randori* and *kata*, I was asked by Mrs. Fukuda to take possession of the *densho* and become the new master of the dojo. In all honesty though, I felt that I had neither the necessary skills nor the courage to assume this responsibility, nevertheless, I found it difficult to decline Mrs. Fukuda's earnest request and so I finally accepted, though with some reluctance.

One day, while I was in charge of classes at the Fukuda dojo, a man who claimed to be an expert in the Honden Miura style of jujutsu came on an unexpected visit to our dojo and challenged us to a contest, which I felt we had to accept. He was extremely confident of his prowess and proudly boasted that we were no match for his style of jujutsu. At that time, I was not the most skilled in the Fukuda dojo. I still lacked confidence, so I was naturally a little anxious at the prospect of competing against his team members. If we lost this contest to the Honden Miura School, it would have lowered not only my reputation but also that of our dojo. I asked and received the support of the other trainees and we all agreed on a date and a time for a team contest, with this the man left. On the appointed day our team assembled in the dojo somewhat apprehensively and we waited for our opponents to arrive. However, they failed to show up. The man was obviously a braggart.

I recall another anecdote from my days at the Fukuda dojo. Normally, I did not have a particularly hard time when practicing with Aoki and the other trainees. In the case of Fukushima, however, it was a completely different story. I could not overcome the strength nor disturb the balance of Kanekichi Fukushima no matter how hard or how often I tried. Finally, I resolved that I would learn to throw him somehow or other. After giving the matter a great deal of thought, I decided that a sumo technique might be effective against him. Upon hearing that a former sumo man, Kisoemon Uchiyama, worked at my university dormitory, I requested him to teach me sumo techniques. The sumo throws that I learned from him, however, proved to be totally ineffective against Fukushima. It then occurred to me to research books on western style wrestling, so I went to my local public library in Yushima, Bunkyo Ward. Unfortunately from among the wrestling books available, there did not seem to be any throw that I could use on Fukushima, except one that I thought just might be effective against him since Fukushima was taller than I. This throw was a shoulder wheel or *kata-guruma*. I experimented with it on one of my student friends soon after reading about it and succeeded in throwing him. I also tried it on Aoki with the same result. On my next visit to the dojo, therefore, I challenged Fukushima to a practice, and for the first time in my life I successfully threw him with my newly acquired technique. After many months of trying, I had finally managed to down him. I was overjoyed and felt a great sense of achievement.

(Kano included in this interview some additional comments concerning Kanekichi Fukushima, which Mr. Ochiai recorded as follows.)

3. Kanekichi Fukushima

I heard the following anecdote concerning Fukushima from my former jujutsu instructor, Fukuda. Fukushima was a fish wholesaler at the huge Tsukiji fish market in downtown Nihonbashi, Tokyo. He was a plain, simple man. Since he was the boss, he had a large number of younger men working under him. One evening, he went out for a stroll through the red-light district of Yoshiwara, apparently with no intention of visiting any of the establishments there, but as he was passing one, he was grabbed by the arm and half pulled, half escorted into it. Being a man of sturdy build, he soon struggled free and rushed back into the street. Just then, someone from inside the building threw a cup at him, which hit him on the forehead causing a painful swelling. Understandably, he became enraged. As he left the scene he reportedly yelled, 'You're going to be sorry for that!' He did not go home, but stayed somewhere else for two or three nights and then returned for his revenge. Two men came out of the brothel to confront him. Fukushima attacked them both and kicked them to the ground. He then grabbed the lintel from above the doorway, ripped it off and using it as a weapon, started on a wrecking spree. Because he was in frenzy and so powerful and well trained in jujutsu, nobody had the courage to approach him let alone try to restrain him. Shortly thereafter, the police were called and two or three officers raced to the scene. When Fukushima saw the policemen though, he realized that his anger was not directed at them, immediately regained his composure and meekly put his hands behind his back and allowed them to handcuff his wrists, arrest him and lead him away to the cells at the local police station. The police later investigated his case. They admitted that the red-light district was an unruly area and under the circumstances decided to release him from custody upon payment of a 20 sen fine.

Another incident that I recall was when Fukuda gave us instruction in the application of *kappo* resuscitation techniques. In one instance, as if to quickly revive a victim of unconsciousness, the trainee had to place a hand on his partner's abdomen while his partner lay supine and then strongly push in the direction of his chest. My partner, while I lay down on the mat, happened to be Fukushima, who exclaimed when requested to perform *kappo*, 'I can't do that. Kano's too skinny. If I press him, I'll crush him to death!'

On another occasion, he and his gang of workmen were attending a festival at a local shrine. Since Fukushima was the boss of a large fish wholesaler business, he was obliged to look after the interests of his men. During the festivities, one of his men was attacked and struck by a member of a rival group who was also attending this same event. Fukushima became incensed. He sought out the culprit and threw him to the ground. This incident soon escalated into a furious brawl among members of both groups and quite naturally the shrine authorities took a very dim view of this disgraceful spectacle.

Afterwards, Fukushima felt totally responsible for the trouble that had been caused and was deeply remorseful. For the next several days he seemed depressed. One night, he mentioned to his wife that he was going to visit a shrine. She was so worried over his changed mood and unusual behavior that she secretly asked someone to follow her husband after he went out. He made his way to the bank of the Tamagawa River where he suddenly ran down into the water and then violently struck his head with a piece of rock. Passers-by made an attempt to rescue the unconscious Fukushima, but they were unsuccessful and he drowned.

4. Master Masatomo Iso

Following the untimely death of Master Fukuda at the age of fifty-two, I was, for a time, obliged to assume responsibility for teaching the other students at the Fukuda dojo even though I had neither the experience nor the self-assurance to do so. Despite Fukuda's passing, I had not, however, given up my resolve to become totally skilled in jujutsu, and I was fully aware of the reputation of the famous Iso School of Tenjin Shinyo jujutsu that had been founded by Master Masaemon Iso. His successor was Masaichiro Iso, and although employed as an instructor at the Kobusho, Masaichiro was not a particularly well-known jujutsu man and was reportedly not very successful in contest. He, similar to Fukuda, also died at an early age. The third generation master was Masatomo Iso, who was better known and had been Fukuda's teacher. Iso ran his dojo in Otamagaike, Kanda, Tokyo.

After much thought, I decided that it would be in my best interests to enroll at Masatomo Iso's dojo in an effort to improve myself further in jujutsu. At that time, Master Iso was over sixty years old. Though he no longer practiced *randori*, he continued to give in-depth instruction in *kata,* for which he was a well-known expert. He had appointed two of his ablest students, Sato and Muramatsu, to stand in for him in the *randori* training sessions and therefore I received initial coaching in *randori* from both of them. Because I had trained hard at the Fukuda dojo and had acquired a fair amount of experience, I soon gained great benefit from their further instruction, so much so that I was eventually called upon to become an assistant instructor at the Iso dojo.

Although short in stature, Masatomo Iso was of sturdy physique. Even in his younger days he was noted more for his knowledge of *kata* than for skill in *randori*. Therefore, I did not learn many *randori* skills from him, but I did learn a great deal of *kata* technique. By teaching and practicing with his students, I gained much that I was able to use to my advantage in furthering my skills in *randori* practice. According to Sato, many years ago three jujutsu men from a rival dojo came unannounced to the Iso dojo. The three of them suddenly approached Master Iso and were about to seize him. One advanced from the front, one from the right side and one from the left. Iso anticipated their attacks, counterattacked with *atemi* strikes and in an instant sent all three to the floor. The three would-be attackers were astonished and so awed by their experience that they later sent Master Iso gifts! It is never an easy matter to defend oneself from one determined assailant, let alone three attacking simultaneously. Such *atemi* techniques, however, were Iso's forte.

Another incident concerning Iso occurred as follows. A current member of the Kodokan is Nuitaro Inoue, who now holds a 5th dan grade. His foster father, Keitaro, a former student of Mataichiro Iso, was an assistant teacher at the dojo and well versed in Tenjin Shinyo jujutsu. He regarded Master Iso as his superior and sought advice from him, especially in *kata*. Sato said that on one occasion, however, when Master Iso was demonstrating *kata,* Keitaro suddenly and without warning thrust Iso in the solar plexus with a *bokuto* or wooden imitation sword, but surprisingly Iso remained unmoved. From this, we can deduce that despite advanced years, Iso must have been in excellent physical condition.

In my days at the Iso dojo, some thirty or so fellow members practiced regularly every evening. Because the two other assistant teachers were sometimes absent, I alone had to lead the training sessions. Unlike today, the main practice session in those days was not considered to be *randori,* but *kata*. Customarily we did *kata* training first, followed by *randori*. Having to do *randori* nightly with thirty or so partners proved to be quite an arduous task for me. I used to leave for the dojo after an early dinner and arrive back home late, sometimes well after 11 p.m. Because my legs hurt so much following the hard training and exercise sessions, I had difficulty walking in a straight line and occasionally stumbled and fell down. When I now recall those far off days, I am somewhat surprised that I did not succumb to illness.

I recall making a very big mistake on one occasion in particular. For several consecutive nights, a stranger came to the dojo merely to sit and view our training sessions. One night, after we had finished practicing *kata* and had almost finished a hard session of *randori,* the stranger unexpectedly asked Master Iso if he might join in our practice session. Upon receiving permission to do so, he asked to borrow a jujutsu suit, and then approached me and requested me to practice with him. I agreed. We bowed and began *randori*. I attacked with *tomoe-nage*. He sidestepped my attack and as I lay on my back, he pounced on me and secured a hold-down. Since he was of ordinary build, not especially strong or skillful, I should have been able to escape from his hold without much difficulty. Because our training session was almost finished, however, I was by then almost completely exhausted from the earlier exertions. He, on the other hand, was fresh on the mat; I therefore had little energy left in me with which to make my escape. While I was in the midst of attempting to do so, however, he abruptly said, "Thank you" stood up, left the mat and the dojo, never to return. That occurrence was a mistake on my part. If I had not been so tired, I would surely have thrown him and had the better of him in any groundwork encounter. It was quite reckless of me to have accepted his challenge on such an occasion. It was an error of judgment that beginners often make, for when we are extremely tired, we do not always exercise the wisest of decisions. In my youth at the Fukuda dojo I was often warned by Master Fukuda about my being careless. That particular experience drove home Fukuda's message and proved to be a valuable lesson.

5. My Study of Kito Jujutsu

As time went by, the visits to the dojo of both Sato and Muramatsu became much less frequent. I, however, still very keen, continued my practice of Tenjin Shinyo jujutsu regularly every night. In June 1881, Master Iso died. For the second time, I was left without a jujutsu instructor and I again had the difficulty of finding yet another master. It so happened that one of my student-day elder acquaintances was Masahisa Motoyama, who in 1878 had become one of the first students to graduate from the Law Department at Tokyo University. Although we were in different departments while students, we were, nevertheless, members of the same baseball team and became close friends. Ryusaku Godai and I were pitchers for the team. Masahisa Motoyama and one of the other students were catchers. Accordingly, Motoyama and I associated with one another and often went hiking and rowing together. I later learned that Motoyama's father was a well-known expert in Kito style jujutsu and that he had formerly instructed at the Kobusho. Naturally my curiosity was aroused and for this reason I hit upon the idea of learning from his father, Master Motoyama, the Kito style of jujutsu, a style that was unknown to me.

Because his father was by then quite elderly, he taught only *kata*. He was no longer able to practice or even willing to teach *randori* skills. Owing to my persistence though, Master Motoyama finally relented and agreed to introduce me to a good instructor whom he had known from his younger days. He told me that this man's name was Tsunetoshi Iikubo and that he had taught for a time at the Kobusho. Shortly thereafter, I was introduced to Iikubo from whom I subsequently took lessons in Kito style jujutsu. Surprisingly to me, the Kito style was very different from the Tenjin Shinyo style jujutsu to which

I had by then become well-accustomed. In Tenjin Shinyo, there are a range of strangulation techniques and groundwork hold-downs. On the other hand, the Kito style, rather than hold-downs, comprises a wide range of effective throwing techniques. There are a number of sacrifice throws together with several foot and several hip throws that I had never seen before. I therefore soon discovered more ways of throwing an assailant to the ground. When I met Master Iikubo, he was already over fifty years old. Nevertheless, he was still remarkably skillful in *randori* and had stamina enough to train hard. At first, and for some considerable time afterward, I was no match for the formidable *randori* skills of Master Iikubo. Also, the Kito *kata* that I learned from Iikubo was somewhat different from that of Tenjin Shinyo style *kata*. Since I found the wide variety of Kito jujutsu throwing techniques so fascinating, I studied them painstakingly and practiced them relentlessly.

6. University Days

Besides my jujutsu training exertions, I also put a fair amount of effort into my studies at Tokyo Imperial University. In those days, there were four main subjects of study for students in the Literature Department; namely, politics, economics, philosophy and Japanese literature. Majoring in politics and economics, I eventually gained a degree. I also studied philosophy and English literature with the many English-speaking foreign professors who were engaged there. A number of my fellow students later in life distinguished themselves as professors, politicians and prominent businessmen.

For the first three years of my four-year course, I concentrated on politics, economics and philosophy. Immediately following graduation, I enrolled as a special-student on a further one-year course in philosophy. In January 1879, while still involved in my studies, I was persuaded to apply for the position of lecturer in politics and economics at the peers' school, Gakushuin. My qualifications proved to be acceptable and my application was subsequently approved. Oddly enough though, some of the students whom I was to teach were much older than I. There were two courses being taught at Gakushuin, one using foreign-language textbooks and the other using only Japanese-language texts. Among my students enrolled on the course studying the foreign-language textbooks were a number of prominent nobles who were also members of the Japanese Diet.

During my student days I lived in lodgings, but soon after becoming a lecturer at Gakushuin, I decided to move out and set up house for myself. Shortly thereafter, I was requested to coach some students in preparation for their university entrance examinations. Because the number of my private live-in students quickly grew, I needed to move to larger premises. As a result, in February 1882, I made a decision to rent rooms in a temple named Eishoji in Shitaya, Kita Inari-cho (present-day Higashi Ueno, Daito-ku, Tokyo). I chose two rooms for my own personal use, one of which I used as a study. Other rooms were for the use of my students. The largest room available we used as a jujutsu dojo, not only for my academic students but also for others who came wishing to learn jujutsu only. I engaged Master Iikubo to teach both *kata* and *randori*. Among my live-in students at that time, were Tsunejiro Tomita, currently 6th dan grade, and the very skillful Shiro Saigo.

An anecdote from those days concerned the problems stemming from the loose floorboards that were directly below the mats of the dojo. Repairs were eventually needed following the months of constant pounding by falling bodies. One night, Tomita and I decided to fix them. Tomita crawled underneath the temple verandah while I held the lantern. The head priest was worried. He complained that the vibrations resulting from the crashing of bodies during our practice sessions had made the memorial tablets in the room next to the dojo fall to the floor. Not only that, but some of the roof tiles had become dislodged and had fallen down too. Finally, the head priest seemed afraid that we would eventually wreck the temple completely and asked us to stop using the main room as a jujutsu dojo. After much thought, I decided to have a new and sturdy purpose-built, twelve-mat dojo constructed next to one of the gates in the temple grounds, this I named Kodokan.

7. Sporting Activities

As a direct result of my constant training in jujutsu, I had become much stronger physically. In my younger days, I had tried other forms of physical exercise such as gymnastics, running, rowing and hiking. The sporting activity that I engaged in most often, however, apart from jujutsu, was baseball. Although rowing is helpful to some extent in building up one's physique, if one does not live close to a large lake or river, the traveling back and forth in order to row each time is not only a waste of valuable time but also quite fatiguing. Moreover, if one rows irregularly, it is of little help in achieving muscular development. Therefore, mainly because of the inconvenience of travel that I experienced when I lived in downtown Kanda, Tokyo, I considered rowing to be an unsuitable activity for me personally.

My fellow Tokyo University students and I formed a hiking club and from time to time we went on trips to the mountainous areas that surround Tokyo. We usually went hiking on Sundays and on public holidays. Looking back now, it proved to be a tiring experience and I do not think that it benefited us much physically. Playing baseball involves mainly throwing the ball and batting, but these physical exertions exercise few muscle groups. The whole body is not exercised a great deal. In addition, one needs a large open space and two teams to play the game properly. During this time other teams are prevented from playing on the pitch. In a typical game, only a few of the baseball team members are physically active: the pitcher, batter and to some extent the basemen. Although the basemen have a few activities to perform, the fielders are, for the most part, generally inactive. Thus, the benefits to be derived from such physical exercise for the team as a whole are in my view very much limited. Although baseball can be fun to play, it is not really a suitable activity for vigorously exercising all of the body's muscle groups. When I went rowing, I usually rowed on the Sumida river from Ryogoku to Mukojima and then on to Senju-Ohashi. That was a day-long activity. Sometimes, of course, it is good to go rowing for relaxation. However, rowing does not have much of a beneficial effect on the harmonious development of one's general physique. Therefore, to my way of thinking, for exercising all of the major muscle groups of the body, there is no physical activity more beneficial than vigorous jujutsu-type training.

8. From Jujutsu to Judo

In my younger days, I tended to be somewhat irritable and at times very hot tempered. After a few years of training in jujutsu, however, I found that my health had improved. I had become calmer as a result of much greater self-control. I also concluded that the same spirit necessary to prevail in a life or death struggle against an enemy on the battlefield could be similarly applied in an attempt to overcome difficulties that we often have to face in our daily lives. The training necessary to acquire competent fighting skills that enable one to defeat an enemy in battle is, in a sense, also very valuable as intellectual training. Traditional jujutsu techniques were devised for the most part solely for the maiming or killing of an enemy, not in anyway for anything positive morally, intellectually or physically. I concluded, however, that after modification, many of these same jujutsu techniques could be performed in a less dangerous manner, could be of a practical nature for modern-day life and could be of value in the exercising of one's body and in the improving of one's mental faculties.

Besides the Tenjin Shinyo and Kito styles, I studied the techniques of other schools of jujutsu. I came to realize also that martial arts training could be used as a potent force in the pursuit of self-perfection. From a variety of jujutsu styles, I decided to adopt the most effective techniques and add some of my own ideas. By founding judo, therefore, I had created my own system of physical and mental training. It also occurred to me that I should not keep this knowledge to myself alone, but that I should teach it to others worldwide.

At that time, there were still a relatively large number of people nationwide with an interest in a variety of traditional martial arts. However, since some were averse to living in the past, as it were, they thought it better to give up practicing such outmoded activities. Thus, martial arts started to lose their former popularity, particularly the unarmed styles of jujutsu. In an effort to reverse the decline in their incomes, some jujutsu masters began staging exhibition matches. They issued challenges to sumo wrestlers and to practitioners from other jujutsu schools. The admission fees that they charged spectators helped to boost their salaries. In this way, the world of martial arts started to be transformed into an entertainment business and thus the true character of these arts was altered and degraded radically. Partly because of this changing situation, the former popularity of jujutsu as a participant activity began to wane further. When I began teaching martial arts in earnest, I did not instruct traditional jujutsu as such, but an art that was based on a deep and far-reaching spirituality. Since jujutsu had by then largely fallen into disrepute, I purposely did not use the term jujutsu at all, but thought it better to use a different name; the one that I selected was 'Kodokan judo'.

The essential spirit necessary for one to prevail in a fight, which largely determines the outcome, has important implications for life. In judo, initially the student is taught the 'do' or way to live one's life, in other words, a lifestyle, and later he learns the appropriate fighting skills for the practice of judo. When considering a name for this new activity, I purposely did not change the name completely for I retained the meaning of 'ju' which means yielding or flexible and added 'do' the path or way of life. Thus, the name I chose was judo.

The word 'judo' had, in fact, been used earlier, by one of my former jujutsu masters. Moreover, the word judo had at one time been used by the popular Jikishin School, which was based in the Izumo-no-Kuni region. However, they seldom used it. They most often referred to their particular style as jujutsu, Yawara or Taijutsu. I was, therefore, the first to popularize the use of the term 'judo'. Similarly, the name kendo was sometimes used in the days of kenjutsu, a martial art which has been popular since ancient times. Today, however, the name kendo, like judo, has come into much wider use.

In recent years, instead of referring to my art by the official name of Kodokan judo, most people now simply refer to it as judo. However, the term Kodokan judo is special in that it has wide application and deep significance. The institute that I named Kodokan is, therefore, the place where the art of judo is taught. If I had merely wished to teach a martial art, I would have perhaps named my dojo Renbukan (institute for martial arts practice) or Kobukan (martial arts institute) or perhaps Shobukan (military institute). I especially avoided the use of such terms though. The chief reason that I chose the name Kodokan was that the 'do' of judo is the fundamental 'path' of life to which the skills are applied.

(This account, given by Kano, takes us up to May 1882. In the following three articles, some of the information was supplied to me by others.) Based on his ideology, in 1882, when Kano was twenty-one years old, he established his Kodokan at Eisho Temple, in the Shitaya area of Tokyo. (Mr. Ochiai)

9. The Inspiration for 'Seiryoku Zenyo'

While a student at the English Language School, Kano lodged at the house of his former headmaster, Shosaku Hida, who was a close friend of Kano's father. Hida was also engaged as a secretary at the Ministry of Education. Boarding together at the headmaster's house was one of Kano's classmates and rival, Kumazo Tsuboi, who later in life became the head of Bunka University. On one occasion, as part of their summer vacation geography homework, they were instructed by their teacher to commit to memory the names of principal cities on a map of the United Kingdom. On their way from school, they decided to compete to see who could learn the most names of British cities and also read the greatest number of books during their summer vacation. When they returned to Mr. Hida's house after their summer break, it transpired that Tsuboi had read more books and had memorized more than twice as many names of British cities than had Kano.

Although Kano admired Tsuboi's powers of retention, from another perspective, however, Kano was not disheartened at being bettered by Tsuboi. Kano said that he had read the number of books that he had intended to read and at the same time had also been fully committed to his physical training routine; on the other hand, Tsuboi had achieved better results than Kano, but Tsuboi's summer activities had been limited to reading and to the memorization of names on a map. While Kano admired Tsuboi in some ways, he had no wish to emulate him completely.

Later, Kano was enrolled at Kaisei School. One of his classmates was Naoharu Shiraishi, who in subsequent years became an eminent civil engineer and a prominent Seiyukai Party politician, active in the Diet. Shiraishi was a very capable student, but unlike some of his fellows, he never lost sleep by secretly studying after lights out. On the contrary, he always had a full night's sleep, took time for regular exercise and did not seem to study to any great excess. Nevertheless, he always did well in his examinations. In addition to Shiraishi's intellectual prowess, Kano quickly realized that there must be some other reason for his impressive scholastic performances. This puzzled Kano. He therefore decided to observe closely Shiraishi's daily routine. Occasionally the teachers curtailed lessons by ten minutes or so. Most of Kano's classmates often wasted this time by playing around. Kano noticed, however, that Shiraishi always used such occasions profitably by either revising his lessons or by preparing for forthcoming ones. On another occasion, a one-hour lesson was cancelled. Again, most of the students spent this time in idle chatter, but not Shiraishi, as usual he quietly proceeded with his studies. Kano quickly perceived the fact that one of the main reasons for Shiraishi's success in examinations was that he never seemed to waste time, not even the shortest periods, but used his time on these occasions to utmost effect. Kano was impressed. Thus, this experience greatly influenced Kano and when he too had odd moments of free time, he did likewise and used his spare time in a much more constructive manner than he had done previously. It was this observation of Shiraishi that gave Kano the germ of an idea for his now famous motto, *Seiryoku Zenyo*, which became one of his favorite messages and which he conveyed to his students so enthusiastically throughout his life.

10. Kano's Attitude Toward Book Learning

During his days at both Kaisei School and later at Tokyo Imperial University, Kano devoted more time and effort in attempting to strengthen both his physique and his willpower, than to reading. Along with like-minded fellow students, he frequently engaged in sporting activities as a means to help him achieve these aims. Sometimes he and his fellows would go on day-long hiking trips to the rural areas surrounding Tokyo. On those occasions, Kano's favorite topics of discussion were said to be how to strengthen one's character and how to develop a strong spirit of perseverance. He would often stay up till late at night when immersed in discussions on these, his pet subjects.

Kano said that one could learn and thus benefit from the knowledge contained in books at almost any time of life. The first priority when young was for one to develop a strong character. If a man does not read much, book learning will understandably have little influence on him. On the other hand, if he reads books avidly, he is likely to fall into the trap of merely adopting the successive opinions of the writers of such books. What is vitally important is for one to read with comprehension in order to fully digest the knowledge contained in the book. Kano believed that reading books indiscriminately was not a good thing either. He often said that we must think and then read, read and then think. In order to develop insight, we need to be focused on our subject and to read carefully rather than superficially and extensively. He also said the following: "If I had concentrated solely on attending lectures and studying books, perhaps I would have been able to widen my knowledge much more by the time of my graduation. However, I wouldn't have been able to achieve my objective of developing a strong character nor would I have been able to improve the quality of my life. In retrospect maybe my methods were not the best, but I firmly believe that they were of some value."

11. Regrets

During his university days, Kano recalled one matter of lament in particular. He said that he had become too absorbed in reading books that were unrelated to his major studies. The gist of his comments is as follows:

"In the majority of cases, textbooks designated as most suitable for university students at each stage of their progression are chosen for course work, therefore, students should study all subjects specified. If one does not study these subjects at the appropriate time, the opportunity for reaping optimum benefit from such books may well be lost, for there is usually little inclination for one to study them later on in life. Knowledge contained in such prescribed books forms the bedrock for further advanced study. If we wish to build a tower, we must start by constructing a solid foundation. Education is based on this same principle. First, the student needs to acquire a firm grasp of fundamental knowledge and later add to his store. Students like or, as the case may be, dislike a variety of subjects. By leaving the choice of texts up to the students' discretion, some no doubt would probably neglect the basics of the discipline and though completely ill-prepared, rush headlong into the field of advanced study.

"I passed university examinations in all my required subjects, but in retrospect, I now regret that I didn't concentrate more on my foundation course reading in these subjects. I sometimes skimmed through bulky volumes, such as Hamilton's *Metaphysics*, (Here, I believe that he is referring to his days at Kaisei School.) and many others, but now on reflection, I benefited little from reading of this kind. If I had limited my energies to the study of books equivalent to my level of scholastic attainment, I think I would have profited much more, for if we read difficult books too early, we cannot gain much knowledge from them even though we may study them very hard. In addition, my favorite hobby subjects, such as astronomy and so forth, which were totally foreign to my required reading, I tended to read far too much. Only half understanding a subject is of little use. In fact, nibbling at knowledge that had little relevance and neglecting the books that I should have studied at greater length is now a matter of much disappointment. It is usually while studying foundation course subjects that one's aptitude for one's major study gradually comes to the fore. For this reason, one should focus on one's principal course of study, for if we neglect sufficient study of foundation course subjects, there's a danger that when we proceed to more specialist studies our knowledge will not be solidly based. We therefore need to pursue a broad range of foundation subjects. By doing so, our ideas directed towards our major subject will be more firmly targeted and through such methods we will gain in confidence."

12. The Kodokan Oath

Among my earliest students at the Kodokan in 1882, were several non-residents and a few who actually lodged there, among these was Tsunejiro Tomita, who now holds the rank of 6th dan. In those days, however, his name was Yamada. Later, a family named Tomita adopted him and his name was changed. He was my first judo student. Shortly thereafter, in August 1882, the now famous Shiro Saigo became a student of mine. Born Shiro Shida, he took the name Shiro Hoshina for a time. Afterwards he was adopted by Tanomo Saigo, and in order to resurrect the Saigo family line, he was obliged to assume the surname Saigo. Among my former non-resident judo students were some who eventually gained black belt status and who are now members of the House of Peers. These politicians include Naruyasu Okeguchi and Sumifumi Arima, chamberlain to the imperial family. Arima became principal of a junior high school and later a senior high school. In addition to teaching them judo, I also taught both Arima and Okeguchi at Gakushuin. Nobody imagined that my former classmate, Kojiro Tatsumi, of all people, would take up judo training under me, but he did, though I have to admit he gave it up shortly afterwards. Later, we graduated from Tokyo Imperial University together.

All students admitted to the Kodokan in the early days were obliged to swear an oath of allegiance to the Kodokan. The oath consisted of the following five articles:

1. From this day forth, I promise to persevere in judo and shall not quit training for any frivolous reason.
2. I shall not bring dishonor on the Kodokan.
3. I promise that I will not divulge to others any of the secret arts of judo by either visual or verbal means to any person or persons whatsoever without authorization from the Kodokan.
4. I shall not instruct others in the art of judo without authorization from the Kodokan.

5. I shall abide by all rules of the Kodokan dojo both before and after receiving a Kodokan judo teacher's license.

Although some twenty or so students attended my judo-training sessions from May to December in 1882, only nine in fact signed their allegiance to the oath. Later, in 1884, the wording of the oath was revised. From 1882 until the official enactment of the revised oath in early 1884, there were still only nine students who had signed it. Before ratification, however, the majority of practicing students ceased their training, leaving only the original nine signatories to the oath. Thus, from 1882 to 1884, the number of students who undertook judo training was far greater than the number who actually consented to sign the Kodokan oath.

Shiro Saigo
(1866-1922)
Celebrated Exponent
of Yama-arashi

Tsunejiro Tomita
(1865-1937)
Kano's first judo student

13. Kosuke Shirai

After Genzo Murata, a native of Yamaguchi Prefecture, returned to Japan from his studies in America, he served as principal of Koriyama Junior High School in Fukushima Prefecture and later as principal of Hikone Junior High School. In his younger days, I gave him instruction in both English and judo. Later, Murata and I studied classical Chinese together at Mishima Juku. One day, Murata introduced me to Kosuke Shirai, a very colorful character. Shirai, senior to Captain Yamagata, was a loyalist, and a strong supporter of Emperor Meiji. Before the Meiji Restoration, Yamagata was leader of a commando force, and I heard tell that Shirai was commander of the Southern Commando Corps. Shirai and Yamagata were good friends and both had been very actively engaged in governmental affairs. In addition, Torio Koya and Goro Miura, both elder than I, were also Shirai's close friends.

Shirai was a heavy drinker and often became unruly and sometimes even violent when drunk. Nevertheless, he was an interesting man and because he usually got on well with my students, Murata asked if Shirai might stay with us at the Kodokan for a time. Since my students and I wished to learn from his experiences of life and especially about the important historical events that had taken place in Japan prior to the Meiji Restoration of 1868, I gave him a room in Eishoji and we treated him as a guest. We were often awed by his daring military exploits and when sober he was usually polite to both my students and to me. On the other hand, during his drinking bouts he sometimes became troublesome not only in our company but he also caused problems on his visits to other people's houses. When on one occasion he was invited to Captain Yamagata's house, he apparently yelled at Mrs. Yamagata and ordered her to bring him more rice wine. Even so, Yamagata as usual, forgave him for his outbursts and in fact treated Shirai well, giving him presents, such as new clothes on occasions. I was impressed with the camaraderie of their relationship. His other acquaintances, such as Torio Koya and Goro Miura were also always generous towards Shirai.

At times, Shirai was an amusing character. Although there was no direct personal relationship between us, I nevertheless respected him as one of my seniors. When drinking though, he became a nuisance and would occasionally strike my students without the slightest provocation. He sometimes attempted to hit me also. Even though I had respect for him as a military officer,

I would not allow him to behave in an offensive manner. Shirai would often yell, "Kano!" and stride towards me as if to strike a blow. At such times, I would quickly grab him in a non-threatening manner merely in an attempt to restrain him. Shirai was then bewildered, and would then mutter something such as, "Kano is great, great." No matter how drunk he was, he never actually landed a blow on me and would always listen to anything that I might say to him on such occasions. Only by the mere act of restraining him for awhile, I found that I was often able to exert much influence over him.

In one discussion I had with Shirai, I recall asking him how one could win the hearts and minds of a great many people and gain their trust. He advised me to help those in trouble and distress by imagining myself in their situation. I thought his suggestion convincing then, but now I only partly agree with him. I believe it natural that if we help a man in difficulties, he is likely to be grateful and think well of us. However, performing such actions as indicated by Shirai will not enable us to gain respect from the populace at large. I think it important for us to help others willingly, and with compassion, but not solely with a view to gaining their favor and confidence. Man is not almighty, if a man immediately and instinctively sacrifices himself on behalf of everyone he sees in trouble; eventually he will become less able to serve society in general.

We have to understand, therefore, that we cannot always help individuals in adversity, even though we may have strong feelings of sympathy towards them. Moreover, when we do help others, we should do so as an expression of empathy, not just as a way of trying to gain their support. I think, however, that Shirai was partly right, and as a result of his suggestions I think that I became more compassionate and willing to help those in difficulty. While Shirai stayed with us, he informed us about key political events that had occurred during the Meiji period. Therefore, all things considered, despite the fact that he troubled my students at times, I think that from an educational perspective he had quite a positive influence on them.

14. A Fruitless Search

I have another recollection of those far off days. The first time that I set up home for myself was when I went to live in rented rooms at Eishoji temple. At the time, my father was also living in Tokyo, in Fukagawa, Saga-cho.

Because this relocation was the start of my living independently, he visited me one day to see how I was managing on my own. I had engaged the services of a cook, an elderly woman who came in to prepare meals for my students and for me. Since the cooking that she did for us was rather bland, I decided to treat my father to something special, something a bit tastier. I had heard that there was a popular eatery in the neighborhood that served the most delicious broiled eels. I therefore invited my father to dine there. He accepted my invitation and we left for the restaurant. However, no matter how much I searched, I was unable to find the location of the restaurant, I became lost and reluctantly had to give up. I then decided to take my father to another restaurant that I had also heard good reports of, but again I failed to find that one, too. Finally, after the long trek, we returned home tired and a lot hungrier. Naturally, I was very embarrassed for taking my father on such a wild goose chase. Strange as it may seem, however, this incident seemed to please my father somewhat because it proved to him that I did not indulge in luxury of any sort.

Many years later, in 1912, I went to France and there became aware of these same sentiments that my father had shown towards me. I had tutored Yotaro Sugimura when he was a student. He is currently serving as a roving ambassador and Assistant Secretary-General to the League of Nations. When I met him in Paris, however, Sugimura was engaged as a secretary at the Japanese Embassy. Because he admitted to me that he had scant knowledge of the tourist sites of Paris, in his stead Ambassador Viscount Ishii agreed to guide me around the city. Sugimura maintained that he had been so absorbed in his work and therefore had not allowed himself to be distracted by any other activities whatsoever. I was glad to hear of this, and it enabled me to understand well the reason that many years previously my father was uncritical of me, even though I had caused him some consternation by not being able to find the best restaurants in our neighborhood.

15. The Warehouse Dojo

Until February 1883, I lived in lodgings at Eishoji temple in the Shitaya area of Tokyo, following which, thanks to Genzo Murata, I was able to move into more comfortable accommodations. At that time, Murata had begun to have a tract of land that he owned in Fukushima Prefecture cleared for cultivation. Although I had no direct dealings with his business undertakings, I did give him some financial assistance. Since Murata wished to open an office in Tokyo for the Nihon Kosan Company, which was carrying out the above-mentioned project, he asked me if I would be interested in finding a suitable house for rent that we could share. I readily agreed to this proposal. We searched and eventually found a vacant residence in Imagawa-koji, which was owned by the famous botanist, Yoshio Tanaka. The nameplate of the Nihon Kosan Company was subsequently attached to the front door and we moved in shortly thereafter. Although the house had an adequate number of rooms for the accommodation of my students, there was unfortunately no room that was large enough for a moderately-sized dojo.

I should also explain here about my English language school, Kobunkan. I opened the Kobunkan in 1882, in Ichiban-cho, central Tokyo because I wished to promote the academic abilities of my students in addition to their physical conditioning. Later, I moved the Kobunkan to Minami Jimbocho, then finally to Imagawa-koji. I closed this school some seven years later, in 1889, when I left Japan on my first extensive European trip for the purpose of educational research. After moving from Shitaya to the rented house at Imagawa-koji, as above-mentioned, we had no dojo. However, when I moved the Kobunkan to Minami Jimbocho, I discovered that there was an empty warehouse next door. We soon made enquiries, agreed to rent it and arranged to convert this solid stone structure into a dojo of sorts. Some of my students whom I taught there later distinguished themselves in life. Masaya Suzuki, for instance, became leader of the giant Sumitomo financial and industrial combine, Manjiro Inagaki became a diplomat, and Eizaburo Kamei a statesman.

Although we used the warehouse as our Kodokan dojo for only about one year, I have many anecdotes to tell of those days, some amusing and some not so. The main problem for me was in trying to attract beginners to take up judo in such cold, bleak and altogether dank surroundings. Although I had confidence enough in my ability to teach judo, I was regarded by most people as a mere inexperienced graduate. Moreover, it was at this time that jujutsu was being increasingly shunned by the public at large as an outdated activity, and because many people did not know that judo differed from jujutsu, the reputation of judo was suffering much the same fate. Quite naturally, few wished to learn the largely unknown art of judo from an equally unknown instructor. I gave special consideration to the few students who did join my dojo though, and did my best to try to ensure that they would find judo of interest and thus become enthusiastic trainees. If I had been able to have the use of a fine purpose-built dojo, there would probably have been more students join. The warehouse afforded a practice area of only ten tatami mats, and there were square pillars here and there. A few ruffians occasionally turned up at training sessions and tended to throw their opponents with full force. I was always afraid that they would collide with the pillars and thus cause injuries. This was a matter of growing concern to me, for if my students suffered injuries, they would no doubt regard judo as a dangerous activity and drop out. Genjiro Amano, who died recently, was until a few years ago the manager of a hotel in Osaka. He trained in judo in those days at the warehouse dojo and studied at my school. He was physically very strong and practiced energetically with me, but he was inclined to use his strength to excess, so much so that I sometimes had difficulty in coaching him without injury to himself!

Another problem I had was how to arrange training sessions at times that were suitable for the majority of trainees. Short periods at specified times for training proved to be unworkable; so, I expanded the timeframe of these sessions, allowing trainees to come for practice at any time from 7 a.m. until 12 noon on Sunday mornings, and from 3 p.m. until 7 p.m. on other days. However, because there were so few trainees, these sessions proved to be far too long. If I was not in the dojo and there was nobody else of high grade there to lead the practice session, the students soon left and went home. For this reason, some trainees eventually stopped coming to the dojo all together. To encourage them to attend and to retain their interest, I had to be ready in the dojo so that they could practice with me no matter what time they arrived. On weekday afternoons, I was more willing to wait for my trainees to arrive, but on cold Sunday mornings at 7 a.m. I was much less inclined, being unsure that they would even show up at all.

If for some reason I was unable to attend at 7 a.m. on Sunday mornings, I would arrange for Shiro Saigo to act as my replacement. Therefore, Saigo often had to endure the cold and wait alone until someone arrived for practice. Even now, I can clearly remember the problems we encountered in those far off days. When Saigo and I were both there, we would practice together; our feet numb with cold. Since Saigo was little more than a beginner at that time, even before I was warmed up he would soon become too tired to continue the practice. Nonetheless, after taking intermittent rest periods, we practiced again and again, and eventually stopped only to find very often that our feet were still numb. In those days, life was difficult for me in many ways; however, when witnessing the splendid present-day development of the Kodokan, those memories now seem somewhat more pleasing and my efforts over the intervening years worthwhile.

16. The Kami Niban-cho Dojo

In February 1884, I moved into a rented house in the grounds of Daishakyo, a Shinto shrine at Kami Niban-cho, Tokyo. This house was quite spacious and had seven or eight rooms as I recall. Although the rooms were suitable for the accommodation of my students, none was large enough for the practice of judo. Nevertheless, we decided to convert an eight-mat room near the lobby into a dojo. Even though I had few students at that time, the room was far from appropriate. We therefore removed two built-in closets at one end of the room so that we could extend the mat area, but we had another problem, in the center of the room there was a pillar. This posed a danger, especially during *randori* practice sessions, so I wished to have it removed. Naturally, the owner did not share my enthusiasm for judo and was not at all pleased to hear of my suggestion, but eventually we managed to gain his assent and the pillar was removed. The room was still far from ideal, but at least we had the use of a reasonably-sized and much more importantly, a safe practice area.

At first it was again difficult for me to attract newcomers. As time went by though, the student membership started to increase steadily. Unlike the two smaller houses that I had previously rented at Imagawa-koji and at Minami Jimbo-cho, here we had the convenience of a dojo actually on the premises. This allowed us greater freedom to practice each afternoon from two or three o'clock until quite late at night if we so wished. As my students improved in skill, a few were able to stand in for me and lead the training sessions in my absence. I therefore let my trainees practice at any time they wished, from two o'clock in the afternoon to eleven or sometimes twelve midnight. It was a matter of regret, however, if there were no partners available for a keen member who had specifically turned up for practice. If the non-resident students did not have partners to practice with, they soon left the dojo rather than wait for someone to arrive. In an effort to deter them from leaving, I gave instructions for my resident students to wait already wearing their judo suits. I was, shortly after that time, raised to the post of full professor at Gakushuin. Upon completion of my daily lectures there, I would hurry back to the dojo each afternoon in order to teach judo. While waiting for students to arrive, I often read books in the dojo. In an effort to keep warm during cold weather, I wore a judo suit, with a thick *Haori* top coat slipped over my shoulders, I was, therefore, immediately available for practice. When my students arrived, I would carry my small desk and place it in the next room, remove my *Haori* and partner them for practice. I advised my resident students to do all they could to encourage the non-residents in an effort to maintain their interest in judo for if we failed to do so, they would quit. Among those whom I taught at that time and who later in life achieved fame was Takejiro Yuasa, commander of the warship *Sagami Maru*, which was part of the fleet that enforced the blockade of Port Arthur during the Russo-Japanese War of 1904-1905. He joined my dojo in September 1883. In October of the same year the well-known scholar of English Literature, Masujiro Honda, became a student of mine. Another man, who is now on the Kodokan Board of Trustees, Itsuro Munakata, became my student in February 1884. In August, the current highest dan grade holder, Yoshitsugu Yamashita, joined my dojo. In October of the same year, the manager of the Kodokan, Junichiro Seki, also became a student. In November of 1884, a member of the Kodokan committee, naval officer Jiro Nango, came for judo instruction.

At that time, I recall that I had a great difficulty. Fumihiko Yokosei, a secretary at the Finance Ministry and a popular journalist requested that I teach him judo. He was older than I and indeed the eldest member of the Kodokan. Since he was a man of some importance, we were glad and indeed honored to have him join our dojo. I therefore hoped that he would continue with his training. Because of his advanced years though, he asked me to teach him *kata* rather than *randori*. I taught him the Tenjin Shinyo *kata* that I knew well. He was fit for his age and practiced long without resting. Nevertheless, I always had concern when teaching him, since I had to be very careful that he did not injure himself. He attended practice sessions for quite a time, but eventually it became apparent that he was not making as much progress as he expected and finally he quit. My efforts were thus unrewarded. Nonetheless, that episode impressed upon me the hard work and dedication that my associates and I were continuing to put into our development of the Kodokan. This was borne out shortly thereafter because the number of new students sharply increased and our ten-mat dojo soon became far too small. Fortunately, there was adequate space for the construction of a new twenty-mat dojo in the grounds surrounding the house.

The Kodokan custom of annual, month-long, mid-winter training (*Kangeiko*) was instigated at the Kami Niban-cho dojo. This practice, observed by adherents of the ancient martial and cultural arts, had been largely discontinued after the Meiji Restoration. However, I decided to resurrect the tradition of *Kangeiko* in a further effort to cultivate in my students a spirit of tolerance both physically and mentally not only in response to the harsh coldness of mid-winter, but by extension, to encourage this same spirit when faced with other difficulties in life. I held *Kangeiko* training before breakfast, from 4 a.m. to 7 a.m., for a period of thirty consecutive days.

17. Educational Responsibilities

So far I have commented much on judo matters, I now wish to say something about education. In January 1882, as above mentioned, I was engaged as a lecturer of economics and political science at Gakushuin. From March 1884 until 1887 I was appointed professor of economics at Komaba Agricultural School (present-day Tokyo University of Agriculture). In July 1884, Gakushuin, which had been until then a private-run college administered by the Peers' Club, became a state-run institution. Following this significant administrative change, I continued my lectureship at Gakushuin. Tateki Tani, a well-known army lieutenant general, was appointed as principal. Because he was a confidant of Emperor Meiji, the atmosphere his appointment created was somewhat more oppressive than that when General Nogi was appointed principal some years later.

Besides my teaching duties at Gakushuin, in April 1885, I was also obliged to assume other duties. In addition to my lecturing, I had to deal with the general affairs of the college and I was also responsible for the administration of two departments. This administrative responsibility proved to be quite demanding mentally. It was around this time that I started to do research on education in a broader sense, since I had, from the days of my youth, a very strong interest in education. In December 1885, Tani was appointed as Minister for Agriculture and Commerce, and in his stead, Keisuke Otori became principal of Gakushuin. Shortly thereafter, there was again a reorganization of both the curriculum and the administration. Besides my promotion to a professorship, I was later appointed, with the approval of Emperor Meiji, to the position of principal of Gakushuin.

18. The Origin of Kano Juku

Soon after I moved to Eishoji; I opened a preparatory school, Kano Juku. Similar to the Kodokan at that time, I had but few pupils. Some were children whom friends and relations had requested me to teach and to supervise during their studies, together with a few children who approached me for help with their lessons in exchange for their assistance both in the housekeeping chores of the Kodokan and in the teaching of judo. At first, I made no strict rules with regard to the lessons. I gave instruction in a relaxed and informal manner. As the number of students increased, however, and because their ages and requirements differed, it became necessary for me to lay down rules, formulate a policy and to set academic goals. My private preparatory school was not named nor did it have any official opening ceremony as such, it simply grew and grew and was referred to by the neighbors as 'Kano Juku'.

Although I made a few rules for students to follow in the Shitaya and Imagawa-koji days, I did not draw up officially in writing any guidance on academic policy. I occasionally called students together and merely gave them advice or simply gave impromptu tuition to them individually. In 1884, however, after moving to Kami Niban-cho, Kojimachi, I introduced the first formal policy. Some children, whom I was asked to teach, were from wealthy families, often with a governess and servants to tend to their every need, and as such, most of them were selfish, weak-willed and spoiled. Some others, mainly as a result of a lack of discipline at home, fell into the practice of idling away their time. Therefore, their parents requested me to teach them in a strict manner and make them study hard. From among my students, I observed that many of those who had had bitter experiences early in life, such as those who had to lodge at the Kodokan since they had no alternative accommodation, naturally developed strong willpower and a bold temperament and in due course often became useful members of society after reaching adulthood. I also came to the conclusion that it was necessary for those children who, being closely attached to their parents, were apt to be overly protected from the hardships of life and therefore needed to experience a rigorous regimen of education at my school.

19. School Rules

The rules that I introduced at Kano Juku were not cast in stone, but were altered occasionally in keeping with our changed circumstances. The first rule that I laid down at Kami Niban-cho was that bedtime would be at 9:30 p.m. and wake up call time would be at 4:45 a.m. on the dot. The youngest boys, however, were sent to bed earlier, at around 9 p.m. Each morning, one boy would rise earlier than his fellows in order to ring the wake-up bell at 4:45 a.m.

My belief in those days was that a man should train himself to wake up on time. Because of this idea, I gave instruction that each boy in turn would assume the duty of waking up his fellows. The night before, the boy whose turn it was to carry out this duty had to ensure that the alarm clock and the lamp were in place by his bed in preparation for his getting up on time the following morning. This custom ensured that the other boys could relax and rest well since they were fully confident that they would not be allowed to oversleep the following morning.

Immediately upon rising, the boys were required to tidy their own rooms. They then took turns in sweeping the lobby, the garden path and removing any discarded litter from the section of public road directly in front of the Kodokan. The scheduled periods of study were always followed by judo training. In addition, rest times were also fixed. While studying, the boys were required to wear *hakama* and to sit on the floor in formal *seiza* style. At meal times the students took turns in waiting on the instructors. During the meal there was usually a mutual exchange of views, the instructors would question the boys and they in turn would question their instructors in seeking their advice. The boys were obliged to answer the door and bid farewell to visitors when they left. I operated a strict rota system, so that each boy took his turn in doing these and the many other menial household duties. While the boys from wealthy families paid for tuition, those from poor families were unable to do so and so were given free tuition. Nevertheless, I insisted that those from privileged backgrounds and those underprivileged should always be treated equally. There was no favoritism. When the boys went outdoors, my rule was that they had to go out together, as a group. They were not permitted to go out alone, unless they had some special reason for doing so. They were not allowed to visit their parents without my approval; however, those who lived in

Tokyo were permitted a Sunday home visit for a fixed period twice a month.

I accepted students under the condition that while they remained under my tutelage, I was to be their sole guardian. Sometimes I refused to allow them a home visit even at their parents' request. Among my first group of students at Kami Niban-cho, there were some who distinguished themselves later in life, Masujiro Honda became a well-known English language translator and interpreter, Itsuro Munakata an artist, Takejiro Yuasa a naval lieutenant commander and Shiro Saigo a judo star. Another of my rules was that students had to wear *hakama* throughout the day, except in the dojo, when judo suits were worn. The elder boys were permitted to receive pocket money from their parents, but not the younger. The boys were all given daily necessities, such as soap and towels, as required. They were not allowed to buy cakes nor were they permitted to bring food items from home. The one exception to this rule was our weekly tea party when cakes were served.

I had my students train in judo daily in the dojo. Each Sunday everyone gathered there for my lectures on topics often focused on morality, important guidance to be followed in life and advice on ways to achieve success. Also on Sundays, I encouraged students, except those visiting home, to go on walking tours to the countryside surrounding Tokyo. Even on the coldest winter days the use of *hibachi* (charcoal braziers) in their rooms was forbidden. I kept them busy with the daily chores of cleaning their rooms, the oil lamps, the bathrooms and so forth. The only exception to the daily household jobs was that they were not required to cook any meals.

I believe that a disciplined regimen is an excellent method for the development of character and that all the rules I introduced were a means towards attaining this goal. The reason for my adoption of such a spartan lifestyle was as follows. My paternal grandfather had at one time given instruction to the chief priest at Jomyo-In, a Buddhist temple of the Risshu sect in Ueno, Tokyo. Because of this relationship, the chief priest sometimes called on my father. I also, on occasions, had opportunities to visit Jomyo-In. On such visits I noticed that the daily regimen for the monks at this temple was severe. The monks were permitted only one meal a day. They rose at 4 a.m. each morning to start the day's disciplines, which included cleaning the inside of the temple buildings and sweeping all leaves from the temple grounds. The cleaning process was so thorough that though old, the temple and the precincts were always neat and clean; all equipment was placed orderly and was well cared for. Following these observances, I quickly realized the benefits that could be derived for my students' character development by adopting these same customs of early rising and thorough cleaning duties.

20. New Year's Day Ceremony

The act of contributing something for the benefit of society is exemplified in the New Year's Day Ceremony, which I introduced to my Kodokan students in 1884. As I recall, it was performed like so: I first poured from a decanter a little Toso (sweetened rice wine), specially prepared for New Year's Day, into an extra large sake cup. I did not drink the Toso, but passed both the decanter and the partially filled sake cup to my most senior guest sitting next to me. He also poured a little Toso from the decanter into the large sake cup before passing them to the person sitting next to him. Everyone present repeated this ritual around the assembled group until eventually both the decanter and the sake cup were returned to me. All the while they were being passed around; nobody sipped a drop of Toso. The second time around, no more Toso was added to the sake cup and again nobody drank from the cup as it was passed from hand to hand. When the sake cup came back to me on the third occasion, I took the first tiny sip of the Toso, but drank much less than the amount that I had initially poured into the cup. In like manner, each person sipped less than he had initially poured into the cup; therefore, after the third revolution around the group, some Toso remained in the sake cup. This cup containing the remaining amount of Toso was then placed on the *kamidana* as an offering to deity.

The action of pouring Toso into the sake cup is emblematic of work. The sake is not drunk, but is passed to one's neighbor and then to the next person and so on around the group. This signifies the act of bequeathing something of value to others. Nobody drinks, but each in turn adds a little Toso to the cup before passing it to the person seated next to him. The second time around, again each person passes the cup to his neighbor, but without pouring any more Toso into the cup. On the third revolution, I take the first sip, but drink much less than the amount of Toso that I had poured into the cup initially. Each person, one by one, does likewise, thus, much Toso remains in the cup and is saved. This act signifies collectively putting something by for the future benefit of all or by extension, for the future benefit of society. Later, when I had a much larger number of students, the second round was omitted. Later still, when more students had joined us, two sake cups were used, one passed to the right-hand side and the other to the left simultaneously, therefore, eventually both sake cups were returned to me.

This ceremony is meant to represent the fact that Kano Juku students overcome the difficulties of life by developing the virtues of perseverance and self-denial that one often has to foster for worthwhile gains, especially so when seeking to help others. I therefore introduced this ritual in order to symbolize my own way of cultivating a young person's mind and spirit along these lines.

21. The Vital Principle of Randori

I should now like to return again to the subject of Kodokan judo. By the time I opened the Kodokan in 1882, all the well-known recognized masters of Tenjin Shinyo jujutsu had died. Even though I had already begun teaching jujutsu to others, I still continued to receive instruction in Kito jujutsu from Master Tsunetoshi Iikubo until around 1885 or 1886. When I established my dojo, Iikubo was over 50 years of age, nonetheless, he was still fit and much more skilled than I, particularly so in *randori*. That was why I wished for his further coaching in *randori* as well as *kata*. At that time, however, a change came about in my throwing techniques resulting from the progress that I had made in my own research. I would here like to give a detailed account as to how this significant event occurred.

Normally, during our *randori* practice sessions, Iikubo, being superior in skill, threw me often. One day, however, I believe it was in the year 1885 during a bout of *randori*, I managed to throw him for the very first time. Although Iikubo tried quite desperately to throw me, he was unable to do so for the duration of our practice session, whereas my techniques on him were repeatedly successful. Since he was a noted expert, he seemed a little surprised and looked somewhat puzzled, obviously wondering why such an unusual occurrence had happened on that particular day. I concluded that my success was undoubtedly the result of my study of *kuzushi*, or methods of breaking my opponent's balance. I was thus able to use to my advantage the knowledge that I had so recently acquired. I had noticed the direction in which my opponent's balance could be broken when he reacted to certain moves that I made. In particular, I concentrated on disturbing my opponent's balance a split second before attempting to throw him. Following this study, the original six directions that I taught for upsetting the opponent's balance were augmented to eight, which I later incorporated and taught to my students at the Kodokan. By causing the opponent to move in any one of these eight principal directions, it is possible to disturb his balance.

From my studies at that time, it became apparent to me that in whichever direction the opponent is pushed or pulled, the result is always the same – his balance is disturbed. I can break to the rear the balance of a man of quite powerful physique merely by placing my hand on his chest and pushing, or should I grip his jacket lapel and pull, his balance will be broken to the front. If, however, my opponent is as heavy and as strong as I, and I push him, at the same instant that he pushes me, our competing forces will cancel each other out and his balance will not be broken to the rear. Likewise, if I pull him the instant that he pulls me, again the result is stalemate. However, no matter how strong my opponent is, should he pull me at the same instant that I push him, his balance will be immediately and completely disturbed to his rear. If my opponent pushes my chest, and I, at the same time step back to maintain my balance while pulling his lapel, he will undoubtedly stumble, fall or step forward in an effort to regain his balance. Thus, by skillful timing of these actions of pulling and pushing, it is possible for me to upset my opponent's balance. I thus came to realize this important judo principle in which I can exploit my opponent's reactions to my advantage. It is only by seizing the opportunity the moment that the opponent's balance is disturbed that one's attack will most likely succeed. One should, therefore, attempt a throwing technique in the same direction in which the opponent's balance is momentarily unstable.

As mentioned above, one can break the opponent's balance in any one of eight directions; namely, both directly forwards and backwards, directly sideways to the left and to the right and diagonally to both the rear left and the rear right corners, also to the front left and right corners. Therefore, the opponent's balance may be disturbed in any of these eight directions depending on the degree of force that I apply to my opponent's body. Naturally, there may be other times when the opponent's balance is broken midway between any of these eight principal directions. Disturbing the opponent's balance can be achieved in any direction, but as a general rule it should be broken in the direction that the opponent is offering no resistance or, if offering resistance, in the same direction that his resistance is directed. Because some of my students had become quite skillful, I practiced with them often and experimented with a number of throwing techniques, thus, eventually gaining the necessary knowledge that enabled me to unsettle Iikubo's balance and to succeed in throwing him.

22. The Kito Jujutsu Densho

When I first mentioned to Master Iikubo that I had devised a variety of methods of breaking the opponent's balance and by utilizing my opponent's immediate reaction to my initial hand movement, I attempted to throw him in the direction of his reaction; Iikubo said that my conclusion is valid. He further added that he had no more to teach me and that it would be better for me to continue with my study of throwing techniques by practicing with my students. He also said that we should no longer do *randori* together, thus from that day forward, we never practiced again. Nevertheless, I did continue to study *kata* under his guidance and to receive his advice. Shortly thereafter Iikubo presented me with a license certifying me as a master of Kito jujutsu together with a jujutsu suit and the *densho* that a master confers on his student following his gaining master proficiency.

When one makes a detailed comparative study of traditional jujutsu with Kodokan judo, big differences between the two systems soon become apparent. For example, jujutsu masters have mentioned that there are more leg throws and hip throws in the Kodokan judo repertoire than there are in most of the traditional styles of jujutsu. The essential point of difference though, is mainly in the methods of upsetting the opponent's balance. These tactics are unique to Kodokan judo. No matter what technique is to be applied, only after successfully disturbing the opponent's balance should one pursue one's attack.

23. The Purpose of Kodokan Judo

Let me give a brief explanation of the aims of judo, and mention in particular events occurring around the year 1887 when I had finalized creation of the art. Since the very earliest days, the lectures that I gave to my judo students were focused on the following topics: how to develop one's physique, how to achieve success in contest, how to cultivate wisdom and virtue and how to apply these principles in one's daily life. Methods for developing one's physique are derived from the physical education aspect of judo training, while contest skills are derived from the martial art aspect. Moral self-improvement may be attained by exercising self-restraint, by the acquirement of knowledge and by applying the judo spirit of perseverance in seeking to overcome one's difficulties. Thus, my ideals of judo are based on the physical development of the man, trained to excel in skills which will enable him to perform well in contest. In addition, I expect judo students to make full use of the knowledge, principles and worthy ideals gained from their efforts in the dojo in order to help them lead satisfying and worthwhile lives. To begin with, muscular development to excess is not necessarily a desirable attribute, but rather physical flexibility and agility together with swift and skilful movement better enable one to either defend or attack, as the case may be. One should always be conscious of the desirability of maintaining high moral standards, of using all opportunities to increase one's store of useful knowledge and of adhering to these practices in one's daily life outside the dojo. These then are the ideal goals that should be aimed for by the truly dedicated judoka.

When, as a young man, I opened the Kodokan, I stressed the above teachings to my students almost every day. Looking back now, perhaps owing to my youth and inexperience, my methods were somewhat immature and I regret that I was unable to influence all of my judo trainees; nevertheless, I was most sincere in my intentions and the principles were the same then as they are now. My teaching of *randori* was related to the above ideals and I believe that the *randori* practiced then was very much closer to my ideals than that I see commonly practiced today.

24. Deterioration of Randori

There are two main reasons for the deterioration in the way that judo is practiced today. First, there is the increasingly competitive nature of present-day judo. Contest judo events were initially introduced as a means of helping to stimulate a greater interest in judo training among students. At the Kodokan, there are now monthly grading contests, in addition to the biannual Red and White team competition that is held every spring and autumn. Naturally, in order to decide such bouts, specific rules had to be devised. Since Kodokan instructors cannot always be on hand to carry out the many refereeing duties, any judoka may be called upon to act as a contest referee, therefore, contest rules had to be both easy to comprehend and to administer.

At the end of a contest, however, it is not always a simple matter to decide the winner. Contest rules should of necessity be brief and uncomplicated so that those other than Kodokan instructors can understand and interpret them without difficulty. The rules governing current competitive judo seem to have adversely influenced the posture that many pupils adopt when engaged not only in contest but also in their regular *randori* practice bouts in the dojo.

The second reason I give is as follows. Because of the recent great proliferation in the number of judo trainees, we do not yet have enough well-trained instructors capable of teaching the correct way of doing *randori*. This dearth of instruction is the chief reason for the prevalence of wrestling-type judo that I see engaged in by many present-day students. The correct way to practice *randori*, which was taught in the early days of the Kodokan, has not been taught to the majority of today's trainees. This has resulted in an increase in the 'strength versus strength' or wrestling type of practice, which is contrary to the correct method of *randori* practice.

25. Correct Randori Posture

Although an increasing number of beginners now have fewer chances of learning to do *randori* in the correct manner, they should, nevertheless, take careful note of the higher-graded skilled judo men they see practicing in the dojo and endeavor to do all they can in future to instill in themselves the correct methods. Therefore, I should here like to define some important points to bear in mind when practicing *randori,* whether it is for physical training purposes or for martial arts training practice. First, what is the best posture for one to adopt? The pose of the learner, who juts out his chin, leans his upper body forward and rigidly tenses his arms the whole time is far from the ideal. Normally, one should not tense one's body when standing in natural posture, for it greatly restricts the free and speedy motion of the neck, upper body, arms and legs. The ideal stance is one that enables the judo man to give instant and fluid command to all bodily movement.

In the case of martial arts training for when one's life is at stake, it is crucially important that one be fully on guard and capable of immediate and speedy movement in response to any expected or unexpected attack that may be made by an assailant. In the case of regular *randori* practice at the Kodokan, the beginners are instructed to hold the opponent's lapel with one hand and his sleeve with the other hand. Although beginners need to be taught such grips, there is no necessity for these grips to be maintained throughout the entire practice session. Most of the time, the opponent's sleeve and lapel should be gripped lightly. If one does not do so and grasps very firmly, one is again hampered by being incapable of instant, totally free and quick action.

Provided the above advice is borne in mind, learners will come to realize the folly of maintaining a rigid posture and one will see a reduction in the number of trainees who needlessly tense their muscles throughout *randori* practice, for this is both tiring and a waste of energy. Eventually, as the beginners gain in experience, they will learn to appreciate the merits of choosing an upright boxer-like stance. If one assumes a western wrestler's crouched posture and an assailant attacks one with an *atemi* blow, for instance, it will be difficult to avoid the assault, even if one anticipates the attack. It is in most cases, therefore, much better to adopt an upright posture.

Normally the prime objective in self-defense judo is not so much in striking the attacker, but in throwing him to the ground in order to secure a restraining technique. Therefore, one should not maintain, as in boxing, a wide gap between oneself and the attacker, but endeavor to keep the assailant within arm's length as much as possible. At close quarters, it is, of course, much easier for one to grasp the attacker's clothing, hand, arm or neck. When an assailant attacks by lunging or attempting a kick, one must instantly side step, usually to one's left, since most people are right-handed and right-footed, in order to avoid the attack, brace oneself and respond by advancing towards him. In an effort to draw him closer, normally one should grab his right wrist or his right sleeve, again because most people are right-handed and he may be carrying a weapon, and then pull him forward in the direction of his attacking momentum in order to disturb his balance, before closing in on his right-hand side. Since you should by then have complete control of his right arm by the application of an arm lock, and due to his loss of balance, he cannot strike you. Because of the close proximity, there is little danger of his attacking you with his free left hand or left foot while his balance remains firmly under your control. Moreover, by being so close to him and with him now off balance, the assailant will find it impossible to kick you. Nevertheless, one must still keep very alert at close quarters.

For both martial arts training and for judo practice in general, we must re-adopt the methods of effective *randori* practice that were devised in the early days of the Kodokan.

26. Competitive Judo

I should here like to comment on both the spring and fall Red and White team competition, and on the monthly grading contests. These competitive events were introduced at the Kodokan in an effort to encourage students to train more earnestly. The rules for the Red and White team competition and the monthly grading contests were officially drawn up around 1885. For both events, the contestant's name and that of his opponent are drawn and displayed in the dojo beforehand. The grading contests are held once a month, on a Sunday. At the start of these contests, the lower grade bouts are held first. If a contestant wins, he remains on the mat to face another opponent and should he defeat many of his opposers, he advances against higher and higher graded contestants from the opposing team until he is either defeated or the contest ends in a draw. Thus, the better contest men advance by defeating the less skilled opposing team members. Similarly in the case of the Red and White competition, also traditionally held on Sunday mornings, the expert contest man can progress rapidly toward the end of the line when few competitors take part. However, when there are many contestants on the rival team, his task of defeating many or all of them is made somewhat more difficult.

Since we now live in a different age, it is impractical to compare the situation in the past with that of the present. Today, all participants in the above Kodokan contests are of black belt grade, but in the early Kami Niban-cho days, those taking part in the Red and White team competitions ranged from raw beginners to the most advanced students. Comparing the present-day Red and White team competitors, who number in the hundreds, with the few taking part in the past, causes me to reflect on the vivid memories I still have of those early days.

27. Kagami Biraki

Many judo enthusiasts are now quite familiar with the annual events and customs that were inaugurated at the Kodokan. In an attempt to recruit as many judo students as possible in the early days, I charged them neither tuition fees nor dojo fees. At that time, I suppose that I was influenced more by traditional Japanese custom than by the Western profit motive. Thus, I did not request from my students payment in cash or payment in kind such as foodstuffs or gifts for instructing them in judo. However, whenever a boy made application to join the Kodokan, there was only one stipulation, he was obliged to donate to the Kodokan a pair of inexpensive folding paper fans.

During the first week of the New Year, students would bring *mochi,* cakes of pounded rice, to the dojo in order for us to celebrate Kagami Biraki on the second Sunday in January. Today things have changed, instead of donating a pair of folding fans, newcomers are now charged an entrance fee, but the traditional custom of staging the Kagami Biraki ceremony is still observed. In the early years, students brought me cards and letters containing New Year's greetings. In such manner the Kagami Biraki was held annually at the Kodokan.

Today this ceremony remains largely unchanged from the earliest days. It is held in the morning from nine o'clock until eleven o'clock, usually with many guests present. First, one of the judo masters gives a lecture on judo before the assembly of guests and trainees. Next, several students are selected from among those whom the Kodokan instructors judge to have made the most progress over the past year. They then have the honor, of performing *kata* and *randori* before the assembled gathering together with some of the higher graded judoka. Performers are chosen from among the youngest dan grade holders to the most senior. In earlier times, following the performance, students who lived locally would often donate *mochi* to the Kodokan for use as an ingredient in the making of *shiruko,* a thick, sweet soup of red beans. Slices of *mochi* were also grilled. During the meal, selected students would be called to the front of the assembly to receive their dan grade certificates from me. These newly awarded dan grade holders were usually required to act as waiters in serving dishes to the visiting dignitaries attending the ceremony. Normally, students would receive their promotion certificates on one of four occasions during the year. By far the largest number, however, customarily received their awards at the Kagami Biraki ceremony.

28. Kodokan's First Foreign Trainees

In the years 1885 and 1886, the first foreigners joined the Kami Niban-cho dojo in order to learn judo. Among them were two American brothers named Eastlake. The elder, weighing some 100 kilograms, was an English language teacher, and the younger, of much slighter build, was a trading house employee. Though Shiro Saigo was far shorter and lighter than the elder Eastlake, Saigo was able to throw the hefty American with considerable ease. Because word quickly spread of his mastery over the big foreigners, Saigo became something of a celebrity. Non-judo people in particular were most impressed at the spectacle of such a small man so easily throwing a much bigger opponent, so much so that Saigo's exploits induced many others to take up training in judo. Thus, thanks to the prowess of our superstar, the number of applicants for Kodokan membership suddenly surged.

Also at that time, men from various parts of Japan well known for their skills in jujutsu, including some from as far afield as Bizen City, in Okayama Prefecture, visited the Kodokan and issued challenges to my students. One of these experts was a Mr. Otake, who had trained at the famous Totsuka jujutsu school. Otake, skilled in Yoshin jujutsu, issued a challenge to Saigo. Although Otake had rarely been defeated, Saigo threw him repeatedly with *o-soto-otoshi*. Because of Otake's exalted reputation, news of Saigo's accomplishments became even more widely known through word of mouth and the number of students wishing to learn judo again surged substantially. This was especially so among smaller men. Thus, the status of the Kodokan was again given a significant boost.

These notable events caused me to consider other ways of enhancing the reputation and hopefully bolstering the membership of the Kodokan. For instance, I thought that if I could find youths of large physique, persuade them to join the Kodokan and train them, Kodokan judo would receive even further recognition. Although I had under my tutelage some very skilful judo men at that time, they were all lightweights. What I needed, therefore, were heavyweights to take up training in the art. The big man mentioned earlier, Kisoiemon Uchiyama, who worked in the kitchens at Tokyo Imperial University, was from the coastal Kujukuri area in Chiba Prefecture. It was said that many sumo wrestlers came from the fishing community in that part of Japan. I therefore decided to visit Kujukuri with Shiro Saigo. When we arrived there and questioned a number of people in the area, we were told names of various men. When we met them though, it turned out that the claims were somewhat exaggerated for they were either too old or not as big or as strong as we had been led to believe. Our search therefore proved to be a fruitless one; and we returned to Tokyo greatly disappointed.

29. The Kodokan's First Heavyweight

I continued my quest for strong, hefty youths willing to become Kodokan judo students. This did not prove to be an easy undertaking, however, for I had no knowledge of such a boy. One day, I heard mention of a youth of large and powerful build who lived in Yamato-no-gojo. I was told that he was fifteen or sixteen years old, a hearty eater and fond of outdoor pursuits such as hiking and fishing. Thinking that such an energetic youth might well be just the kind of boy that I was looking for, I decided to call on him at his house. After meeting him, I was impressed; he was certainly big, just as I had imagined him to be. I therefore spoke with his parents and sought their agreement for their son to become my student. After much talk, I persuaded his parents to allow me to bring him to Tokyo to live and to train at the Kodokan. We therefore came to Tokyo. When I introduced him to judo though, he was timid and totally lacked enthusiasm for training. In fact he spent most days crying, saying that he wanted to go home. Finally, because of his age and since there did not seem to be any prospect of his taking up judo training seriously, I relented and sent him back home to his parents. This was another big disappointment for us.

Later, during my travels, I arrived one day at Otsu Station. As I left the train, I noticed a large-framed youth standing on the platform. I approached him and asked him where he was from. He replied that he lived locally. In front of the station there was an inn operated by a Mr. Kobayashi. We went there. The boy's name was Masasaburo Ueno. He happened to be a relative of the owner of the inn. I asked Ueno if he would be interested in going to live in Tokyo for judo training, he seemed enthusiastic and said that he would be pleased to go. I then asked to meet his parents. He left the inn and later returned accompanied by his mother and father. We had a long discussion about my plans for their boy. At long last, his parents agreed and gave their consent for me to take him to the Kodokan for training. At that time, however, I was employed in teaching at Gakushuin and engaged in research. Since I was in the middle of an inspection tour of educational facilities in the Hokuriku area, I was unable to take young Ueno to Tokyo immediately. I therefore arranged a day and a time to meet him at Nagahama Station on my way back to Tokyo following the completion of my tour.

As planned, I met young Ueno at the station on my return trip to Tokyo. I was traveling at the time with Yoshitetsu Daito from Hikone. He was in those days a member of the upper house of the Diet and later became Justice Minister. Because he was from Omi and had been so skilled in judo in his youth, he was nicknamed the Saigo of Omi. We met at Rakurakuen in Hikone and later he, Ueno and I traveled together part of the way back to Tokyo on the Tokaido railroad, which was near final completion. On the last stage of the trip back, near Mishima, there was no steam train service in operation. Therefore, the three of us, each carrying baggage, were obliged to board a small railroad car and with laborers pushing the car from behind, we covered the remaining short distance to Mishima Station. Because there was no further extension of the railroad, we parted company with Daito at Mishima Station. Ueno and I traveled on foot through the highland area of Hakone and later arrived at the hot spring resort of Yumoto. Nineteen-year-old Ueno, weighing some 135 kilograms, found it hard work treading the steep slopes as we made our way through Hakone. Although I am much lighter, I too found the trek hard going. I gave Ueno words of encouragement when seeing him laboring. Eventually we reached the Fukuzumi Inn at Yumoto, where we were able to enjoy a refreshing bathe in the hot spring baths. Following our exertions, Ueno and I had a chance to relax and chat.

A few days later, we arrived in Tokyo. Young Ueno was enrolled at both Kano Juku and the Kodokan where I engaged him in judo training. In those days, both my judo students and my Kano Juku students trained together in judo. Even those students who were not specializing in judo, trained just as hard as those who were specializing in the art. The Kodokan had attracted many new members and there was a lively atmosphere in the dojo. Ueno progressed quickly and despite his great bulk he was fairly nimble on his feet. Nevertheless, he did not prove to be a judo man at heart and thus had no wish to specialize in judo. Instead, he expressed an interest in becoming a businessman. He attended Kano Juku for four years between 1889 and 1893 and afterwards moved to Kobe where he entered a company in order to receive business training. The company, owned by the father of a former student of mine and named Sekitansho Shirafuji, was engaged in the marketing of coal. Later, Ueno joined an enterprise run by a group of foreigners and thereafter, ran his own business for a time. Since he was a man of serious nature, I fully expected him to make a success of his business venture, but unfortunately he died of a sudden illness shortly thereafter.

30. The Passing of My Father

To revert for a moment, I moved from Kami Niban-cho, Kojimachi to Fujimi-cho in 1886. The Kodokan was moved in August 1888. I shall talk about this later. I have several matters that I wish to relate about our days at Kami Niban-cho, however, the most traumatic event for me was when my father passed away.

My father, Jirosaku, was born in Sakamoto in Goushu, Shiga Prefecture, near Lake Biwa. He was the second son of the head priest at Hiyoshi, one of the major Shinto shrines. When he was a student, he studied both art and classical Chinese literature. In his youth he traveled quite extensively and stayed for a time at the Kano household, in the well-known sake brewing district of Nada, near Kobe, where he instructed my maternal grandfather, Jisaku, in the teachings of Confucius. This familiarity resulted in my father marrying the eldest daughter of the Kano household, Sadako, my mother. To perpetuate the Kano name and with a view to carrying on the family business of brewing our Kiku-Masamune brand of sake in Nada, he was adopted by the Kano family and thus took the family surname of Kano. Although my grandfather, Jisaku, had a son, he was at that time too young to run the sake brewing business; my grandfather therefore proposed making my father head of the Kano household. My father, however, declined this offer, preferring instead to set up his own house after marriage and live independently. Nonetheless, in the event of my grandparents' early death, he agreed to act as guardian to the children until they reached adulthood. My grandparents had three daughters and a son named Tokusaburo, who, incidentally, is now a trustee of the Kodokan, and was formerly head of a government enterprise and vice president of the Chosen Bank.

Although my father lived in Mikage after he married, he played no part in helping to run the family business. It was my mother alone who supervised the running of the brewery and employed local workers in the business of producing the *sake*. My father was often away, traveling to Osaka, Tokyo and elsewhere in his dealings with the Bakufu governmental authorities of the day. Before the establishment of the Meiji government in 1868, he was involved in a wide range of business ventures. He received government contracts to build battlements at Hyogo, Nishinomiya and at other locations and also leased his cargo ships. Later, he became an administrator for the Japanese Navy and thereafter, until retirement, was employed as a naval correspondent. He died on September 15, 1885, at the age of 74. His death came as a major blow to me during my days at Kami Niban-cho.

31. The Fujimi-cho Dojo

In 1886, Viscount Yajiro Shinagawa was appointed as Minister Plenipotentiary to Germany. Because a former student of mine, Genzo Murata, wished to study in the U.S., Shinagawa, General Yamagata, Major General Horie and I each made a donation to help cover the expense of Murata's sojourn in America. I was requested to arrange this joint effort in support of Murata and as a direct result of my making such arrangements; I met Viscount Yajiro Shinagawa on several occasions. Later, I became well acquainted with him. He was co-operative and had full knowledge and approval of my strong interest in disseminating the practice of judo and in introducing educational reforms. Just before he was about to leave for Germany, he informed me that he wished to discuss some matters with me.

Shinagawa lived in a large Tokyo property, which was surrounded by spacious grounds, in Fujimi-cho, Ichi Banchi. His residence was both imposing and unusual for the time in that it comprised both Western and Japanese styles of architecture and was expensively furnished. Because he had no wish to lease his property to a tenant, and while abroad, had no suitable person in mind to act as caretaker for his house, he asked me if I would care to live there with my students until he returned from his posting to Germany. However, my students and I were still living in rented rooms at Eisho temple where I employed a woman to cook for us; therefore, our circumstances were not too uncomfortable or inconvenient. His house contained seven large rooms, and as such, it was of ample size for us; nevertheless, on reflection I decided to decline Shinagawa's kind offer mainly because I was concerned that my students would cause damage to his expensive furnishings. He, however, replied that he was not too worried on that account and surprisingly insisted that he did not want to charge us any rent for our use of his property. Nonetheless, I would not have felt at ease living in someone's house rent free. I therefore came up with a solution in which I offered to pay him the same amount of rent that I was already paying at Eisho temple in return for the use of his property. Shinagawa readily agreed and accepted my offer. In the spring of 1886, my students and I moved into his splendid residence. Sometime later, in 1888, I arranged for our dojo at Kami Niban-cho to be totally dismantled and re-erected on a vacant plot of land close to Shinagawa's house.

The three years that we lived at Fujimi-cho proved to be a most important period in the development of Kodokan judo, for until 1889, when I left Japan on my first overseas tour, I carried out much research on judo techniques and taught a host of newcomers. There was, as a result, a significant and rapid expansion in membership. The total number of new candidates that were accepted for Kodokan membership in 1886 was 98; in 1887, 292; in 1888, 378 and in 1889, a huge 605 increase.

32. Judo Experts

The largest number of students enrolled at Kano Juku at any one time during the early days at Fujimi-cho was around sixty, all of whom were required to practice judo daily in addition to their academic studies. Of this number, some thirty or so were in residence at Viscount Shinagawa's mansion. In order to house the others, I rented a nearby property in Ichiban-cho. Those who were specializing in judo included Shiro Saigo, Yoshitsugu Yamashita, Sakujiro Yokoyama, Saburo Toharitaki, Nori Sato and Muneji Kimotsuki. Although a number of Kano Juku students including Itsuro Munakata, Masujiro Honda, Takejiro Yuasa, Katsukazu Tamura, Katsutaro Ota, Tokusaburo Kano and Hidetsuke Oshima, were not specializing in judo, nevertheless, they trained together with, and just as strenuously, as my judo trainees. In addition, there were many other very keen judo students regularly attending who were non-residents, such as Takeo Hirose and Keijiro Kawai.

By this time, the Kodokan had gained a favorable reputation for itself. Because of this, we received an increasing number of requests to engage in challenge matches from rival jujutsu dojos. We therefore had to keep in readiness and although the Kodokan's top contest men were willing to accept challengers from all over Japan, not many actually showed up on contest days. The few challengers, who did arrive, however, were defeated. Partly because of the increasing fame of judo, the National Police Agency authorities decided to call up many of the nation's leading martial arts experts. These included noted kenjutsu and jujutsu men from the southern island of Kyushu. The Kodokan was also notified and requested to send representatives. Neither Saigo nor

Tomita were able to attend, but Yamashita, Yokoyama, Sato, Toharitaki and others agreed to participate.

Among those representing the Kodokan were some contestants who were not first-class judo men, nevertheless, since the police authorities had called upon us, we felt obliged to send the full complement of representatives in response to their request. The competition proved to be quite tough. The most closely watched contests that day were those involving Kodokan representatives and those from the famous Totsuka Yoshin School of jujutsu. Most of our men performed throwing techniques well, but in mat work encounters, some of them were often in difficulty. This occurrence was a loud wake-up call for us and we later carried out an urgent review and further study of ground work techniques.

33. Kodokan Ascendancy

Before the 1868 Meiji restoration, Hikosuke Totsuka's students were widely regarded as among the nation's most skilful jujutsu men. After the restoration, his successor, Hideyoshi Totsuka, trained many more students who also became leading exponents of the art. The best of the Totsuka practitioners at the time were those in training at the head dojo in Chiba Prefecture, near Tokyo. By 1887, however, the fledgling Kodokan was also beginning to establish a modest reputation for itself nationwide. This increasing fame again came to the attention of the National Police Agency. In *1888, a contest showdown was called for between 15 representatives from the Kodokan and 15 from the Totsuka Jujutsu School. Two teams of ten men competed. In addition, individuals contested against jujutsu men of other schools.

Among those who represented the Totsuka School were two of their most able men, Taro Terushima an excellent tactician, and Teisuke Nishimura. Terushima fought Yoshitsugu Yamashita, Nishimura faced Sato and Kawai contested against Katayama, apart from two or three draws, surprisingly all the remaining matches were won by the Kodokan's representatives. Even though my students had shown improvement in skills, I did not expect them to win by such a wide margin. I think the favorable result was a reflection of their fighting spirit. Despite the Totsuka School's high reputation, my students had carried the day and thus proved themselves to be far from inferior.

Incidentally, warders employed at the Chiba Prison received instruction in jujutsu from the Totsuka men. Following these contests, the Governor of Chiba Prefecture, Mamoru Funakoshi, accompanied by some of Totsuka's leading jujutsu men, visited the Kodokan to attend a lecture on judo training methods. This was followed by Shiro Saigo giving a demonstration of *randori*. Hideyoshi Totsuka was apparently impressed by Saigo's performance and passed favorable comment. When I heard tell of this, I was well satisfied.

Shortly before the demise of the Tokugawa shogunate government, Totsuka jujutsu had reached the peak of its fame. Instructors of the Tenjin Shinyo School and Iikubo of the Kito jujutsu school had lost to Totsuka experts in contests at the Kobusho. Therefore my students, in particular Saigo, who had done so well against the Totsuka men, pleased me greatly. Even now I still have proud memories of those far off days.

Author's Note

Writers give varying dates on which Kodokan judo versus jujutsu contests took place, which leads one to suspect that contests were held on more than one occasion. For instance, Ichiro Watanabe, on page 898 of his historical budo reference work covering the Meiji era, Meiji Budo Shi, states that the Kodokan won these matches and he gives the following two dates: November 8, 1885, and January 1888.

34. Naval Academy Judo

During our Fujimi-cho days, the Japanese Naval Academy was relocated from Tsukiji, Tokyo, to far off Etajima in Hiroshima Prefecture. Hinosuke Arichi was appointed as the new head of this institution. My judo students Takarabe, Hirose and others were senior students enrolled at this academy. Another of my students, Rokuro Yashiro, was engaged there as a teacher. It seems hardly surprising therefore that Yashiro, Takarabe and Hirose suggested to Arichi that a judo department be set up at the academy. Shortly thereafter, Arichi called on me to discuss this proposal and subsequently asked for my assistance in the appointment of judo instructors. I agreed to co-operate in selecting suitable men to teach judo there.

Sometime later a judo department was established and the first two instructors nominated to teach were Yoshitsugu Yamashita and Noritaka Sato. Later other coaches were engaged as instructors, including Yokoyama, Kimozuke and Yoshimura; therefore, the general standard of the naval students quickly improved. Thereafter, a growing number of skilled judo men emerged not only from the Naval Academy but also from a number of other judo dojos that were formed at around the same time, including one at Gakushuin and another at Tokyo Imperial University.

35. European Journey

In 1885, the then principal of Gakushuin, Lieutenant General Tateki Tani, was appointed to the post of Minister of Agriculture and Commerce. His successor at Gakushuin, Keisuke Ohtori, introduced changes to the structure of both the administration and the curriculum. Later, I was appointed principal of Gakushuin and as such I was obliged to accept a much wider range of responsibilities. Although I had only indirect charge of financial matters, I was entrusted with almost total accountability for the management of college affairs. My duties included the appointment and supervision of teaching staff as well as the revision of both the curriculum and study methods.

At the time, I held the view that Gakushuin should provide students with a more comprehensive education than the education offered at other colleges, but on the other hand, it should not become an institute for the creation of aristocratic privileges, separate from society in general. Children of aristocratic families should, as much as possible, be educated along lines similar to those from less privileged backgrounds. In particular, their comprehensive educational progress should coincide with the development of character and refinement of manners. At the same time, I did not think it good for a Gakushuin student to be too far removed from his aristocratic environment. I also believed that samurai families and families with ordinary background should be allowed to enroll their children at Gakushuin, not because of family wealth alone, but qualifications based on merit. In my opinion, all schools educating children of the nobility should adopt a similar policy. Furthermore, I think that even children who are not of noble birth, providing they have the necessary abilities, should be permitted and indeed even encouraged to study overseas. Likewise, those of proven ability not only from the aristocracy but also from samurai families and those of ordinary backgrounds should be allowed to assume teaching posts at Gakushuin. When Mr. Ohtori was principal of Gakushuin, he agreed with me and with his support I made some progress in this regard. Shortly thereafter, however, Ohtori retired and Lieutenant General Tani was re-appointed head of Gakushuin. Later, Tani was called upon to carry out official duties that took him to his hometown, far from Tokyo, and therefore he was unable to attend Gakushuin. I was thus appointed principal in his stead.

Viscount Hijikata, Minister of the Imperial Household, had no objection to my policies and pushed through my reforms at Gakushuin. However, when Viscount Miura was appointed principal of Gakushuin, it soon became clear that we did not see eye to eye on a variety of issues. It goes without saying therefore that the reforms that I had introduced were not to Miura's liking. Apparently, he did not consider me to be a suitable member of the teaching faculty. I am not sure that that was the prime reason or not; however, Miura asked me if I had any desire to travel abroad. The previous year, the Chancellor of Tokyo Imperial University, Professor Kato, had also asked me if I wished to travel to the West, on that occasion, however, I was immersed in affairs at Gakushuin and declined his offer. This time I replied to Miura's offer in the affirmative since it was considered important to observe educational trends overseas. Viscount Miura put my name forward for consideration by the Imperial Household Department. As a result, I was chosen to go to Europe for the purpose of educational research.

Miura was still head of Gakushuin when I returned to Japan on January 16, 1891, however, I had no position to return to and there was no immediate talk or prospects of any institution wishing to offer me a post. Moreover, there was little that I could do to create any kind of job opening. Whenever I decide to accept a position, I maintain a policy of loyalty and do not quit for personal reasons. My experience of academia has spanned more than 40 years; during that time I have never asked anyone to take over any position that I held nor did I ever contemplate transferring to another post. I always spoke from the viewpoint of an educator and expressed my views when necessary; I also dared to be confrontational at times. The only time that I submitted an official letter of resignation to the Tokyo Teachers' Training College was when I tendered my notice to retire as principal in 1921.

I felt that Miura did not need me and although I was not asked to do so, I voluntarily resigned my appointment at Gakushuin on August 19, 1889, since I planned to go overseas the following month. I also vacated Shinagawa's house in Fujimi-cho that I had been renting. The previous year, through the good offices of Viscount Shinagawa and Army Vice Minister Katsuura, we were allowed the use of an army building at Masago-cho, Tokyo, for our dojo. The Kodokan, therefore, was housed for a time in that same building. Students of Kano Juku remained in rented accommodation in Ichiban-cho. Among my students were Shizuyabe Iwanami, Masujiro Honda and Shiro Saigo who were entrusted with the dual responsibility of managing both Kano Juku and the Kodokan during my absence. At that time, the late Taisho emperor was a pupil at Gakushuin primary school. Although Viscount Soga was supposed to be responsible for the education of the crown prince, in point of fact, Soga was under the total domination of Miura.

I traveled to Europe with Takehiko Yumoto, a former professor to Emperor Hirohito. Yumoto was en route to Germany in order to carry out research at the behest of the Imperial Household. We happened to meet onboard ship and so traveled together. In those days, few Japanese journeyed abroad; in fact, we were the only Japanese passengers on the 7,000 ton steamship *Caledonian* that left Yokohama for Shanghai on September 13, 1889. This vessel was the sole ocean liner regularly sailing this route. In Shanghai, Professor Yumoto and I transferred to the *Irawadi,* and on October 15th we arrived at the port of Marseille in France.

36. Return to Japan

Upon completion of my European inspection tour, I sailed back to Yokohama on January 16, 1891. Kano Juku was still located at Ichiban-cho and the Kodokan remained housed in the army building at Masago-cho, Tokyo. Because I had nowhere to live, I stayed for a time at my elder sister's house in Ichibeiei-cho, Azabu, Tokyo. While I had been away in Europe, there had apparently been several requests for my services made to the Ministry of Education by people in Kumamoto, including Kamon Furusho, Koji Kinoshita, Tomofusa Salsa and Seiichi Tsuda. They felt that reforms were needed at Number Five Junior High School in Kumamoto and so had held negotiations with Ministry of Education authorities. They also suggested that I be offered the post of principal of this Junior High School upon my return from Europe. I was thus approached and called upon to accept their offer. At first I declined on principle, stating that I would not apply for the position because Taro Hirayama was still engaged there as headmaster and that he had no intention of voluntarily relinquishing his post.

I was thereupon asked to consider another offer, the position of counselor at the Ministry of Education. Although the Gakushuin authorities had no objections to this suggestion, in truth, I really had no wish to become a counselor. However, Miura was still principal at Gakushuin. We had our disagreements on certain issues and it quickly became apparent that we were not well suited to one another. I therefore reconsidered the offer of counselor at the Ministry of Education and gradually came round to the idea of carving out a new career for myself, and so after much contemplation, I finally agreed to accept the position under Education Minister Viscount Kensho Yoshikawa and Vice Minister Shinji Tsuji. Shortly thereafter, however, Taro Hirayama took ill and died. Thus, the problem of finding someone to fill this important vacancy came abruptly to the fore. Not only was I again approached and encouraged to apply for the position by people in Kumamoto but I was also strongly urged to accept it by Vice Minister Tsuji. Because I was much more interested in accepting the appointment of principal than that of continuing to work at the Ministry of Education, and since I had no worry of having to vie with others in securing this particular appointment, I willingly accepted.

37. Marriage

Before embarking on my first journey overseas, I had been living alone for some time. From several quarters I was urged to consider a number of young women as possible brides. However, one's choice of lifestyle is generally different from that of others; likewise the woman one chooses for a wife should be left to one's own judgment and in the final instance, the opinions of others should be ignored. I was thirty at that time and after some deliberation, decided to seek a wife. My elder sister, concerned about my unmarried status, had already made overtures to her friends and acquaintances and subsequently informed me of eligible young women whom she knew.

Since my sister had also spoken with Kanehiro Takagi's wife about the introduction of a possible bride for me, they in turn discussed this matter with various people and I was eventually recommended to consider a formal meeting with Sumako Takezoe, the daughter of a scholar of Chinese literature, and a former ambassador to Korea, Shinichiro Takezoe, and her mother. As well as my own situation, I took into consideration the circumstances of the Takezoe family and Sumako. Members of both our families, Takezoe and Kano, subsequently met formally and each finding the other acceptable, preparations for our wedding were made. Because Tsuruo Kimura and I had both attended Kinoshita Juku and were on the teaching staff at Gakushuin, the Takezoe family had no doubt contacted him and made enquires about me. Also, Professor Kinoshita's second son, Hirotsugu Kinoshita, had close relations with Sumako's father, Shinichiro Takezoe and with me. Again, these and others were consulted by members of the Takezoe family concerning my suitability.

At the time of our first meeting, my future wife was an undergraduate at Kazoku Women's College. I had known for sometime, Utako Shimoda, the dean of that college. After all enquiries by both families had been completed, it was arranged that Hirotsugu Kinoshita and his wife would act as go-betweens at our wedding ceremony. On August 7, 1891, Sumako and I were married at the house of my brother-in-law, Mr. Yanagi, in Azabu, Tokyo. From the following day until September my wife and I avoided the mid-summer heat of Tokyo and went to stay at a mountain resort in Uraga, Matsuzakiyama. In the meantime, a decision had been taken that I was to become the next principal at Number Five Junior High School, Kumamoto, from the following month. Shortly thereafter; I left my wife in Tokyo and traveled by train to far off Kumamoto in Kyushu.

38. A New Posting

After my arrival in Kumamoto, I quickly discovered that martial arts were not as popular there as I had been led to believe. In former times, before the male heir of a samurai was considered eligible to inherit his father's estate, he had to gain several licenses proving his mastery in martial arts. In spite of this tradition, however, things had changed. There was no dojo at Number Five Junior High School, and so the students had no opportunity to practice judo.

There were, however, some abandoned dojos in the locality where jujutsu had been taught. But, for convenience sake, I wanted to have a dojo constructed on the school premises, exclusively for the use of schoolchildren wishing to learn judo. I lacked sufficient funds to fulfill this ambition; therefore, the only practical alternative I could think of was to convert the storeroom in my quarters into a judo practice area. I arranged for a sturdy wooden floor to be installed and had it covered with tatami. In addition, I placed tatami on the floor of the school waiting room and converted that into a dojo. This enabled me to give instruction at both dojos: one in my living quarters and the other in the school building. Fortunately I had brought with me from the Kodokan, Muneji Kimotsuki, who was able to give me some assistance in the teaching of judo.

Another of my Kodokan judo students, Yazo Noguchi, then a first dan, also accompanied me and helped me teach judo in Kumamoto. He is, by the way, now manager of the Osaka branch of the Dai Ichi Bank. Dr. Susumu Manzawa, Dr. Yoshio Udo and Koremichi Kubo were among the keenest and the best of my schoolboy judo students in those days. Sometime later, in an effort to promote further the spread of judo, I established a Kodokan branch dojo in Kumamoto.

Apart from the Zoshikan, a private school in Kagoshima, there was no other institute of higher learning in the whole of Kyushu. Of all the state schools, Number Five Junior High School was therefore recognized by the Ministry of Education as the premier educational institution. On occasions, I was required to travel on inspection tours to other schools in Kyushu and as such I met many headmasters. At the high school in Nagasaki, there was a medical department that I sometimes had occasion to visit. I there became acquainted with officials active in local government, such as the Governor of Nagasaki Prefecture, Sankyuro Shiba, the Vice Governor, Toraichiro Yokoyama, and in Kumamoto, Tsuruo Kimura, Tomofusa Sassa and Seiichi Tsuda.

Other governors that I knew there included the Governor of Kumamoto Prefecture, Masanao Matsudaira, and Yasukazu Yasuba, the Governor of Fukuoka Prefecture. Mr. Tsuda in particular was very much in favor of a university being established in Kyushu. I was in full agreement with his wishes. Naturally, the building of a university needed vast funding. In order to raise money for the initial feasibility study, Tsuda called for donations from the public domain. Local government leaders Matsudaira and Yasube agreed to provide the proceeds from the sale of lumber that had been felled on Mount Ehikosan. The Minister of Education, Takakore Ohki, was subsequently informed of these developments. Shortly thereafter, however, I was appointed to a new position in Tokyo, and for quite some time no further progress was made in our plans to found a university in Kyushu.

39. Return to Tokyo

In the spring of 1893, I was recalled to Tokyo by the Minister of Education initially for negotiations concerning the management of the ministry's Book Department. The minister had revealed confidential information concerning his predecessor which related to the intended policy of the committee overseeing the accreditation of newly published textbooks. This information, initially disclosed by the manager of the Book Department, had quickly passed to the public domain and had caused much controversy. As a result, the work of the Book Department committee was suspended temporarily. The manager of the Book Department did not believe that he had done wrong; however, since the education minister had leaked this classified information, the manager had taken responsibility for his error of judgment and resigned from his position. A secretary, Mr. Aoki, had been appointed temporarily as replacement manager, but since he was unsuited to the work, I was asked to consider taking over from Mr. Aoki. Admittedly, the task of accrediting textbooks for the nation's schools was a most important one; nevertheless, I did not want to relinquish my post as headmaster in Kumamoto. I learned also on that same occasion that the Minister of Education wanted to introduce reforms to the nation's education system and I was asked to participate in this undertaking as well. Because I wished to see educational reforms introduced in Japan, similar to those that had been introduced in Europe; I had a keen interest in this matter and after much reflection, decided to resign my position in Kumamoto.

News of my decision eventually reached the ears of the local population and had provoked their disapproval. Since I had enjoyed my work and I liked the children, a campaign was organized for the purpose of trying to convince me to change my mind and remain in my post. Although I had mixed feelings about leaving, the duties I had been called upon to accept at the Ministry of Education were of importance for the nation as a whole and after much discussion, I obtained the understanding of all concerned and made preparations for my return to Tokyo. I thereupon appointed Sumiomi Arima, who had been one of my political science and economics students at Gakushuin, as head of the Kumamoto branch of the Kodokan. He later gained a Kodokan 4th dan and secured employment as a schoolmaster at Kumamoto Junior High School. After he had agreed to assume my judo-related responsibilities in Kumamoto, I began making preparations to move back to Tokyo.

40. Ministry of Education Appointment

Upon my starting work at the ministry, I was confronted with a great number of books crammed into two large bookcases. All had to be examined thoroughly and either authorized or rejected for use in the nation's schools. Because of criticism from some quarters that books worthy of authorization were being unnecessarily delayed, there was growing resentment at the slow pace of evaluation.

As a result of these complaints, a shakeup occurred shortly thereafter. Tagama Kawano was replaced by Kowashi Inoue as Minister of Education and Vice Education Minister Yuzuru Kubota was succeeded by Nobuaki Makino. Nonetheless, these administrative changes in leadership did nothing to expedite the appraisal of textbooks because the major problem that we faced was not addressed; namely, that of acute understaffing. Few full-time staff members were allocated to our department and only one or two part-timers were hired to assist us. Formerly, such eminent scholars as Seijitsu Sato and others had supported the department in its work. Because of this chronic staff shortage, we had to do the clerical work of the department as well as our principal regular duties, thus our workload was quite onerous. Eventually, Professor Hiroshi Kurita and other able scholars were called in to give urgent assistance. They often worked alongside us until 2 a.m. and sometimes even worked throughout the entire night. I was young and fit in those days and on occasions I too worked late hours on several consecutive nights in order to finish my allocation of textbooks on time.

While Kawano was Minister of Education, a plan was put before him for reforms to the education system. However, this plan was merely reviewed by Kawano, and little progress was made throughout his time in office. Later, when Kowashi Inoue took over as minister, he gave more positive leadership. Inoue was head of the Imperial Household library and a trustee of Gakushuin when I was engaged there. I therefore often sought Inoue's counsel on educational matters.

There was general consensus among us on the need for educational reform. For instance, I and others believed that university courses were too long. We were, therefore, in favor of streamlining the system so that students could be educated to the same level of proficiency, but over a shorter time frame. Inoue held the view that intensive studies should be concentrated on only after students had entered post graduate school. I agreed with him in this regard. However, the university faction, led by Hamao, was staunchly opposed to our proposals. In fact, apart from a contingent of law department supporters from Osaka, there were so many dissenters that we found it impossible to persuade the majority that there was a requirement for such reforms. Little passionate debate on these issues was generated, and in the end our proposals were not carried through.

41. Concurrent Duties

In January 1893, I rented a large house in Tokyo at Ushigome-sadohara-machi. This residence, owned by Lieutenant General Kurokawa, occupied a sizable plot of land. I taught only my junior students there. All senior students were, as usual, instructed at Ichiban-cho. At that time, Koji Kinoshita was engaged as principal of Number One Junior High School, Tokyo. Since Arata Hamao, chief of the Bureau of Professional Educational Affairs at the Ministry of Education had been appointed to replace Kato as head of a university; Kinoshita was chosen to replace Hamao as chief of the aforementioned bureau. Thereupon, Education Minister Inoue urged me to consider assuming Kinoshita's vacant post of principal at Number One Junior High School.

Because I much preferred academic life to office work, and had more or less finished the task of evaluating my allocation of school textbooks at the Ministry of Education, I willingly accepted his offer and shortly thereafter assumed my duties. Although I was fully prepared to remain as head of the Number One Junior High School for some considerable time, in September of that year, 1893, the principal of the Tokyo Teachers' Training College resigned. No candidate was available for this important position, so even though I was just getting accustomed to my new role at the Number One Junior High School, I was chosen as the successor for this post. Because I had been at the elite school for such a short time and very much wished to remain there, I tried to decline the offer, but pressure was put on me and my efforts proved in vain. The upshot was that I should take up three concurrent duties for the time being: counselor at the Ministry of Education, principal of the Number One Junior High School and principal of the Tokyo Teachers' Training College.

The number of students enrolled at the college in those days was rather low. There were, in each grade, only three classes, totaling some eighty students. The curriculum consisted of humanities, physics, chemistry, and natural history, which made it a relatively small college. I was dissatisfied with the quality of education offered and after I became head, in order to upgrade standards, I had to work hard and accepted a number of added duties. On the other hand, I also had a responsibility to the one thousand or so capable students at Number One Junior High School and I was willing to exert much effort to further their educational aspirations. Although the post of counselor at the Ministry of Education did not require a great deal of my attention, being head of both the Number One Junior High School and the Tokyo Teachers' Training College did require my utmost consideration. On account of the combined heavy responsibilities, I could not continue to hold these three positions for very long.

No candidate, apart from me, was said to be readily available to assume the post of principal at the Tokyo Teachers' Training College. However, there was in fact another possible candidate, Fusanosuke Kuhara, one of the first to graduate from Tokyo University. He was formerly head of a junior high school and later became a professor; he was also totally conversant in the field of education. For me to continue holding my joint responsibilities quickly became an impossible undertaking, therefore, upon reflection the minister decided to appoint Kuhara to head the Number One Junior High School and to place me as full-time head of the Tokyo Teachers' Training College.

Before finally resigning my position as principal of the college in 1921, I actually served three terms in this particular post. The first time, was on September 13, 1893, when I was appointed to serve concurrently as principal, while still fully engaged as head of Number One Junior High School. Soon after, on September 20, I was appointed as full-time principal. On August 20, 1897, I resigned, but on November 19 of the same year, I was re-appointed principal. On January 18, 1898, while still holding this position of principal, I was appointed to the post of head of the Bureau of General Education at the Ministry of Education. On June 20, of that same year, 1898, I was officially appointed full-time head of the Bureau of General Education and thus was obliged to resign my post as principal of the Tokyo Teachers' Training College. Later, on May 9, 1901, I was for the third time appointed principal of the college where I remained until finally relinquishing this post upon official retirement in 1921.

Note by Mr. Ochiai

Kano's tenure as principal of the Tokyo Teachers' Training College was at times a stormy one. He was twice ordered to resign. This was because of the views he held so strongly. He stressed, however, that unbearable pressure was put upon him to force him from office and that in no way did he resign voluntarily. He stood by his principles and argued his case for reform with his critics. On the first occasion, the Minister of Education, Mochiaki Hachisuka, opposed Kano. Nevertheless, Kano was adamant and refused to give in to the minister. This incensed Hachisuka, who then ordered Kano to vacate his post. Kano made no effort at all to seek a new position.

When Kano became head of the Bureau of General Education at the ministry, Kinmochi Saionji was Education Minister. He strongly advised Kano to remain in his post so that he could continue to gain valuable experience as a bureau head. Kano responded by saying that he found his former post of college principal more interesting and that he much preferred it. When Saionji himself also declared his wish for educational reform, the Vice Minister and the bureau chief both voiced their objections to his ideas. Later, the decisions of the authorities were announced and Kano was eventually appointed to the concurrent positions of bureau chief and principal of the Tokyo Teachers' Training College.

Kano's responsibilities, however, proved to be much too heavy. Mr. Sotoyama and Saionji then held discussions which resulted in Kano being appointed full-time bureau chief. Soon after, Yukio Ozaki became Minister of Education followed by Tsuyoshi Inukai and then by Sukenori Kabayama. During Ozaki's term, political party member Morifumi Hakuda became Vice Minister. Hakuda had little knowledge or experience of educational matters and this was a cause of frequent heated exchanges between him and Kano. When Kabayama became Education Minister, tensions further escalated. Because of political party pressure together with the involvement of the vice minister of education, Kano was again asked to resign. Even so he continued to state his views and refused to change them.

42. The Hundred-Mat Dojo

Turning again to the fortunes of the Kodokan, through the good offices of some senior civil servants at the War Ministry, I was permitted the use of a ministry building at Masago-cho, Bunkyo-ku, Tokyo, as a dojo. Because this arrangement was only a temporary measure, however, I was constantly on the look out for permanent premises to house my growing number of students. Shortly thereafter, in 1894, in nearby Shimotomisaka-cho, a large house was put up for sale. Upon inspection, this property proved to be ideal, for not only did it afford adequately-sized accommodation, but the sale also included a sizable plot of land next to the house. I therefore bought the premises and later had a dojo of more than one hundred mats constructed on the adjacent site. I then closed both the Masago-cho dojo in the army building and Kano Juku and transferred all of my students to Shimotomisaka-cho.

Among the dignitaries at the opening ceremony of my new dojo, were Kaishu Katsu, Viscount Shinagawa, kendo master Noboru Watanabe and many others with a keen interest in budo. Demonstrations of *kata* and *randori* were performed and in my opening speech I explained the origins of judo and my plans for its future development. My ambition was to introduce a systematic expansion of Kodokan judo throughout the nation as a whole. Several years before, in 1888, I had outlined these plans to the Imperial Education Association in my lecture on *The Value of Judo in Education*. This lecture was attended by the Minister of Education, Takeyaki Enomoto, and by the Italian Minister and similar to the above opening ceremony, a large gathering of the general public was present.

Note by Mr. Ochiai

Upon becoming head of the Tokyo Teachers' Training College in 1893, Kano moved into the principal's residence at Hitotsubashi, Tokyo. Because of the steady increase in the college student body, more dormitory space was needed, so some students had to be housed in the principal's residence. Kano had an extension added to his house and taught some of his students there. He then had extra rooms added to the Shimotomisaka-cho Kodokan dojo complex and after a time he and his growing family moved in.

His first child, a daughter, Noriko, was born on October 1, 1893, at Sadohara-machi. On June 11, 1895, Kano's second daughter, Tadako, was born at Shimotomisaka-cho. Years later, upon marriage, Tadako wed Professor

Jun Jogenji, of Kyushu Imperial University. Sadly, however, Tadako died following childbirth.

43. Education of Chinese Students

My wife and I occupied accommodations at the Shimotomisaka-cho Kodokan until 1900. In that year my father-in-law, Mr. Takezoe, vacated his house at Goban-cho, Tokyo, and went to live in retirement at his country residence in Odawara, Kanagawa Prefecture. We thereupon moved into his Tokyo house.

Earlier, in 1896, Prince Kinmochi Saionji had been appointed concurrent Foreign Minister and Minister of Education. He was approached by the Chinese Minister to Japan for discussions regarding the education of Chinese students in Tokyo.

Until that time, Chinese students receiving education in Japan studied at the Chinese Legation premises. The Chinese Minister requested Prince Saionji's assistance in having Japanese teachers entrusted with the responsibility of educating these Chinese students. Saionji subsequently discussed this issue with me, but I had no suggestions to offer on how best to deal with this matter. Because I was heavily involved in other affairs I had very little time at my disposal; therefore, I could give no direct help. Nevertheless, I said that if others were selected for the teaching duties, I would assist in an advisory or supervisory capacity. With this understanding, a school building named Kobun Gakuin was constructed in Misaki-cho, Tokyo. The Chinese students were, in due course, transferred from the legation building to Kobun Gakuin. Thereafter the Chinese student body grew rapidly. Later, Foreign Minister of the day, Baron Komura, suggested that either Kobun Gakuin be extended, to accommodate the increasing number of Chinese students, or that an entirely new school annex should be constructed.

However, we were later informed that there was a large house standing vacant in Nishigoken-cho, Ushigome-ku. This property was readily acquired and rented by the school. As a result, the Chinese authorities sent to Kobun Gakuin a further large influx of Chinese civil servants from various regions of China. Because of this expansion, my family and I were permitted the use of a house in the grounds of Kobun Gakuin, so that I was readily available when called upon to attend to school business.

In March 1903, a judo dojo was opened at Kobun Gakuin and was officially designated as the Ushigome branch dojo of the Kodokan. The Chinese students were actively encouraged to join the dojo and were given instruction. In due course, several attained black belt grades.

44. Kodokan Branch Dojos

The first Kodokan branch dojo was the Niraiyama dojo in Shizuoka Prefecture, which opened its doors in October 1887. The second, in September 1888, was at Etajima, in Hiroshima Prefecture. Third, was the Kojimachi dojo, founded in Tokyo, in September 1889. This was followed one month later with the building of a dojo in Kyoto. In September 1902, the Kumamoto Kodokan opened in Kyushu. A branch dojo was started in Ushigome-ku, Tokyo in March 1903. Another dojo was constructed in Shizuoka city and named the Giseikan in July 1908. In November 1918, the first overseas Kodokan branch commenced activities in Seoul, Korea, and in 1919 a dojo was established in Sapporo, Hokkaido.

Largely because of problems in relocating instructors to manage these Kodokan branch dojos, some of them were eventually closed down. Convenience of location resulted in many students preferring to join their local dojos rather than travel to the more distant Kodokan branch dojos. Recently, however, members of the Black Belt Association in rural areas have been making plans to re-open former Kodokan dojos and have ambitions to increase student numbers.

Kodokan Shimotomisaka Dojo
Koishikawa-ku, Tokyo
(in use from 1903-1933)

Kodokan Otsuka Kaiunzaka Dojo, Tokyo
(in use from 1917-1933)

45. Training College Judo

Shortly after I became head of the Tokyo Teachers' Training College, Norifumi Machida, the principal of the junior high school affiliated to our college, suggested to me that Kodokan instructor Itsuro Munakata be invited to teach judo at the college. As I recall, this was around 1894. I agreed to his suggestion and a spare classroom was converted into a makeshift dojo where judo sessions were held. Sometime later, a gymnasium was constructed on site. This provided us with much larger and better equipped facilities for both gymnastics and judo training. The gymnasium became our first real dojo and I therefore named it the Ushokan.

The number of trainees attending judo lessons expanded daily. This prompted me to contemplate the fact that up until that time there was a clear division: judo teachers were trained at the Kodokan and school teachers of a variety of academic subjects were trained at the training college. I concluded that if these future school teachers were capable of also giving judo or other sports-related instruction to their charges, it would perhaps help gain them more respect from their pupils, which would assist them in their becoming more effective in the teaching of their academic subjects. At the Tokyo Teachers' Training College in 1906, I therefore introduced a special course that combined studies in the humanities with gymnastics training. Later, other courses were added in which academic subjects were studied together with training in judo, kendo and other sports.

I thought that this practice would produce not only efficient teachers but would also result in pupils becoming more enthusiastic and motivated when tackling their schoolwork. In practical terms, most of those college students who had received both academic and budo instruction, as I expected, became successful school teachers after graduation. On the other hand, I learned that there were others, once they had qualified as school teachers, gave up budo and concentrated their energies solely on teaching their respective academic subjects. This was often because in addition to giving academic instruction, they had to do much martial arts training in order to keep in good physical condition as well, despite having little time to do so. Some other teachers also gradually lost interest in giving martial arts instruction. It was inevitable, therefore, that their pupils were influenced by this turn of events and they too lost their initial enthusiasm for martial arts and thus gained little from their curtailed budo training experience.

In future, I consider it necessary for more college students to specialize in physical education studies. However, merely possessing such a qualification is insufficient for those wishing to pursue a life-time academic career. Because of this, I decided to extend the physical education course from three to four years and to broaden the curriculum to include ethics, education, physiology and anatomy, together with instruction in gymnastics, judo, kendo and so forth. Although I have to admit now that my plan was not a total success, nevertheless, a fair number of graduates did become proficient teachers.

After the Physical Education Department was established at the Tokyo Teachers' Training College, students were required to train in judo, kendo and gymnastics. The instructors and professors in this department imparted only the essential basic instruction; which of course, was far from adequate. It is my belief that in coming years, an institution more highly focused on the training of specialist educators will be needed.

46. Early Judo Instruction

There has been much progress made in the training of judo instructors since the first Kodokan pioneers were outsourced to regional dojos. In the early days, judo instructors were given no guidance in the art of teaching. The keen newcomers would one day appear in the dojo, join the Kodokan and after practicing for a time, some would become skilful, these members were then chosen and sent out to various dojos to instruct others. The situation is quite different today largely because we have many proficient judo instructors who are graduates of the Tokyo Teachers' Training College.

Although some of the early judo teachers were quite knowledgeable as far as technique is concerned, they received no specific instruction on how to teach judo to others. Despite this deficiency though, they were fairly competent as instructors. On the other hand, there were others who were disinclined to pursue any kind of academic study, but found judo of interest and trained exceptionally hard in order to acquire the technical abilities. While some possessed writing skills, literary or other cultural knowledge, few had any understanding of physiology or anatomy. Therefore, I would have to say in all honesty that neither group was adequately qualified to impart comprehensive judo knowledge to a high degree.

Nonetheless, when comparing them with today's qualified judo instructors, the pioneers, though lacking in certain abilities, had judo spirit, sincerity, enthusiasm and were committed to promoting the dissemination of the art far and wide. I therefore believe that they are fully deserving of our admiration.

Back in the mid 1880s, traditional jujutsu was losing its popularity largely because of its unsavory reputation whereas judo came increasingly to the fore. It must be said, however, that the popularity of Kodokan judo was realized chiefly because judo enthusiasts had brought about a public awareness of its dual value as an excellent means of physical exercise and as a sporting activity. Moreover, if the early judo teachers had had access to the knowledge that is available to today's Physical Education Department graduates from the Tokyo Teachers' Training College, I have no doubt that the general standard of judo today would be very much higher than it is.

When I first sent Kodokan instructors to teach at regional dojos, their salaries of between five and ten yen were lower than those earned by the average company employee of the day. The higher paid judo instructors received some twenty yen a month. The highest salary of all was that paid to Yoshitsugu Yamashita. While coaching at the Naval Academy, Yamashita received twenty-four yen a month whereas those who taught judo at the Police Agency Headquarters were paid no more than ten yen.

47. Instructors' Pay

Judo instructors currently teaching at the Police Agency Headquarters earn more than 100 yen a month and additional income from other teaching duties. Thus, they derive fairly high salaries. Recently instructors at the Naval Academy have been elevated to full-time teaching staff positions and now receive a yearly income of 3,100 yen. Those coaching at the Tokyo Teachers' Training College are in receipt of 1,600 yen per year together with supplementary earnings when teaching at other dojos. Because many of the leading judo instructors these days obtain a monthly income amounting to several hundred yen, their social status has risen as a consequence.

48. The Ideal Judo Instructor

It is my contention that the salaries paid to today's instructors should be higher. Besides having a profound understanding of the technical aspects of judo, the ideal instructor must continually seek ways to improve himself as a teacher. In like manner, therefore, salaries should be increased accordingly. It is, of course, impossible for such goals to be met in a short space of time. Preferably, instructors should train diligently to become expert in techniques of both attack and defense. In addition to being masters in the skills of unarmed combat, judo instructors should also be skilled in the arts of *bojutsu* and *kenjutsu*. They should, moreover, be able to comprehend how one man is able to gain advantage and win in a contest and how another is defeated. They need to have detailed knowledge of physical education, teaching methods and have a thorough grasp of the significance of moral education. Finally, they must understand how the principles of judo can be, by extension, utilized to help one in daily life and how they themselves can be of benefit to society at large.

If the conscientious judo instructor possesses all of these attributes, he should not, in my view, be considered a mere teacher but rather a first-rate educator. On the other hand, should he possess some of these qualities and have knowledge of others, he is perhaps competent enough to hold a responsible position in education. In future I look forward to seeing such capable judo educators graduating from the Physical Education Department at the Tokyo Teachers' Training College.

Over forty-five years have passed by since the Kodokan was founded; during that time there has been great expansion from the first few students in the early days at Eishoji, to today's huge Kodokan membership that numbers several tens of thousands. In excess of ten thousand members have attained black belt grade and there are now both here and abroad more than fifty Black Belt Associations. Other developments include my promotion of academic teachings, writings and lectures on martial arts and on cultural pursuits, on the psychological implications of life or death situations in time of war, on physical training, on strengthening of one's willpower and on the establishment and future development of the Kodokan. In the past there was no extensive and detailed technical analysis carried out on judo. Times have changed. These days judo, similar to traditional *bujutsu*, has become a way of life for many people, and relevant research is carried out. Apart from martial arts, I have also lectured on how the application of the knowledge and virtues associated with sports training can help to improve society at large.

Even though the above-mentioned progress has taken forty-five years to attain, it is, nonetheless, something of an achievement. In future, when the installation of facilities at the Kodokan are fully completed, the facilities will be used to promote further technical judo research while on the other hand the Physical Education Department at the Tokyo Teachers' Training College will become the ideal institution for the proper education of academically qualified judo instructors, I believe. The public today has come to accept the notion that academic courses may also include training in gymnastics, kendo and other sports. Student teachers taking such courses should benefit from the sporting aspect, which is designed to help them develop a sturdy physique, healthy lifestyle, moral rectitude and firmness of character.

49. Additional Judo Instructor Training

The introduction of a regular Tokyo Teachers' Training College course combining liberal arts with gymnastics training was a major course of study offered by the Department of Physical Education. In Kyoto, at about the same time, courses in classical military arts were introduced at the *Bujutsu Senmon Gakko*; the name of this school was later changed to *Budo Senmon Gakko,* which was affiliated to the *Dai Nippon Butokukai*. This school promoted courses principally in judo and kendo, similar to those that were offered at the Tokyo Teachers' Training College. Thus, in addition to graduates from the college, many graduates from the *Budo Senmon Gakko* also became judo and kendo instructors.

Following the Ministry of Education's sanction of compulsory judo and kendo training for junior high school students, a growing number of specialist schools, state and private universities have introduced courses in these disciplines. The standard of skill attained by these graduates is high. As a result, the number of qualified judo and kendo teachers continues to grow markedly. Although these institutions are not yet producing what I consider to be ideal judo instructors, nevertheless, good progress in this direction continues to be made.

50. The Introduction of Judo to Society

Looking back to the time that I established the Kodokan, I recall that I had much difficulty in explaining to the public at large the real essence of judo. Even today there are still many who do not fully appreciate its true value. Compared to the early days though, the general public now has better understanding.

In former times, many styles of jujutsu were popular. Male practitioners of a great number of styles often used expensive weapons such as spears, swords and daggers. Halberds were used mostly by females. Many techniques were performed in a pre-arranged and thus non-violent manner. Such styles were often practiced by those of high social rank. On the other hand, the jujutsu practiced by infantrymen and by males of lower social status tended to be the violent unarmed styles using mainly throwing, grappling and arresting skills. These styles also included blows with the hands and feet, arm locks, leg locks, strangulations as well as methods of restraint. Some of these methods were taught to policemen for use in the apprehending of recalcitrant criminals. Therefore, these styles of jujutsu were mostly based on *bujutsu* battlefield techniques and to some extent were despised by the upper classes as rough and vicious. Because the majority of the general public had little knowledge of the less violent styles of jujutsu, they tended to classify all jujutsu as brutal and believed that all styles were dangerous.

Also, in olden days there were no systemized methods for the teaching of jujutsu. Thus, accidents sometimes occurred, more so during the practice of the unarmed styles, which resulted in practitioners sustaining bruises, joint dislocations and occasionally broken bones. While engaged in groundwork fighting especially, men would often suffer cuts and grazed knees following contact with the floor, strangulation to the point of unconsciousness and injuries resulting from the inept application of arm, leg and especially wrist locks. Of course, jujutsu training was not always a dangerous activity. Nevertheless, because such incidents were fairly common, particularly during the practice of the unarmed styles of jujutsu, I did not want members of the public to associate the violence of jujutsu with Kodokan judo. I therefore carefully examined several styles of jujutsu and chose techniques that were not only less dangerous but were, through dint of regular practice, of some considerable benefit to trainees as a means of physical exercise. This was something that few people were aware of at the time and it was not until many years later that the general public finally came to acknowledge and appreciate this very important aspect of Kodokan judo training methods.

51. Attitudes Towards Judo Training

Attempting to dispel the aforementioned two widely held misunderstandings; namely, that judo is violent and dangerous, has always been a major problem for me. Because of these misconceptions, not many people, viewing a judo practice session for the first time, have the desire to learn it. Some of those who do, however, gradually drop out of class at the beginner's stage for a variety of reasons, and it is never an easy task to dissuade them from doing so or to recruit replacements. On the other hand of course, there are some beginners who quickly become very keen on judo. Nonetheless, despite there being no great difficulty in learning the basic skills associated with ordinary judo practice, the majority of newcomers do not continue with their training past the beginner stage.

Similarly, others give up judo at the intermediate level. Indeed, very few of the keen ones continue their practice of judo throughout life. Some of those who do continue with judo training for many years tend to be the hardy and sometimes the rough, argumentative types, or some of those who are disinclined to pursue scholarly pursuits. More often than not these men take little interest in the theoretical side of judo and overly concentrate their training solely for competition. Correspondingly, many of their fellow trainees dislike such strong emphasis on strenuous competitive-type training and so sometimes quit judo for such reasons.

Often the main criteria for many of the eager ones to persist are not simply a wish to excel in the techniques of Kodokan judo. Their objective is twofold: to develop a stronger physique and to bolster their fighting spirit. If they always wish to practice judo only in an overtly aggressive manner, it would be wrong for the instructor to allow them a totally free hand in this regard. Another tendency that they have is that despite much inducement, some of them seem unable to favor any kind of strong interest in other activities. My belief, however, is that they should seek to do so. They should refrain from becoming involved, as some do, in needless arguments. They should learn to focus their aggressive tendencies solely on their judo training in the dojo and not let it influence their conduct in daily life when dealing with others. However, such self-control often proves far from easy to achieve for some of them.

52. Hardship can be Good Medicine

One thing difficult to comprehend for most people is that the attainment of confidence and a sense of contentment, which can result from mastery of the skills of judo, are to be achieved only after long years of strenuous practice against tough opponents. Similarly in the case of traditional jujutsu, in order to master it well, one must be prepared to undergo harsh training. I experienced such a regimen in my own jujutsu training days, which I think better helped prepare me to instruct, discipline and motivate my own students in judo.

To my way of thinking, those students who are of an aggressive and argumentative nature are of value as subjects of study when carrying out research on the psychology of the judo man. Studying the behavior of such truculent types is an important area of research. Surprisingly though, to make them more inclined to educate themselves, in actual fact, was sometimes not such a great problem for me personally. Of course, there were other times when it proved difficult for me to influence some and to prevent them from arguing among themselves. On the other hand, there were others who were reserved, studious, and persevered with their judo training, though it was not always an easy task for me to make good contest men out of them.

Judging from the tens of thousands who have trained at the Kodokan over the years, a few of those who were sometimes violent and quarrelsome had also committed criminal offences. The vast membership of the Kodokan is composed of people from all walks of life. Having said that, if these few wrongdoers were to be banned from the Kodokan, they would not be exposed to the good influences of the vast majority of our law-abiding membership, and therefore I believe that both their numbers and in consequence their illegal activities would tend to increase. While these men are in training at the Kodokan, they not only receive some moral guidance from their instructors but also a sharp reprimand should they break any of the Kodokan's regulations. The worst offenders are either suspended or expelled from the Kodokan, or they are prohibited from taking part in examinations for promotion. Such sanctions have tended to be effective in placing constraints on their misdemeanors and I believe that these measures have a big impact in helping to reform them. Because of their regular contact with the Kodokan membership in general, these men receive, to some extent at least, proper guidance for the leading of a law-abiding life.

53. Financial Constraints

The long-standing financial problems of the Kodokan, which continue to the present day, cannot be ignored. As many are aware, for the first twelve years of its establishment, from 1882 until 1894, there was no requirement for Kodokan members to pay any fee whatsoever. Furthermore, beginners were allowed the use of a judo suit free of charge. The first ever fee, a charge of one yen for membership enrollment, was initiated in 1894. The motive for its introduction, however, was not to seek any kind of profit, but was merely an attempt to reduce the number of curious onlookers, many of whom wandered into the Kodokan only to stand around ridiculing the efforts of the beginners. It transpired that the initiation of this fee proved to be a good idea because over time it had the desired effect.

Starting from 1904, members were charged a nominal monthly dojo fee of 30 sen. As the Kodokan became increasingly popular, income from dojo fees grew likewise. Thus, for the first time in the history of the Kodokan, part of the expense for the upkeep of the dojo came from members' dojo fees. Despite this turn of events, however, the main objective of Kodokan judo instruction was not compromised by this development. The altruistic goal of teaching a way of life rather than making profit from tuition fees still remained intact. The dedicated students, those who attended regularly, were aware of my efforts and therefore the original Kodokan policy of not charging for judo instruction was maintained. The small amount of income we received from dojo fees made up some of the shortfall in my regular personal expenditures for repair work to the Kodokan facilities. From the earliest days, financial matters proved to be a great concern. When I first sent my leading students to teach at regional dojos for a remuneration of five to ten yen, some refused my request to go for such a small reward, even though the cost of living was relatively low in those days. The instructors who did agree to teach had to pay part of their expenses from their own pockets. Since some of these instructors had insufficient spare cash to cover the total cost of both traveling and new clothing, I was obliged to give them further financial assistance. After finishing their stint of teaching, these instructors would return to Tokyo and often lodged with me, once more at my expense. The next time they went to teach judo, I again had to pay their traveling expenses. Thus, I not only paid almost all of the running costs of the Kodokan but also had to subsidize the living expenses of my instructors as well, which over time became an increasingly heavy financial burden.

These money problems gradually worsened. Since I had remained single for some ten years after my graduation from university I was able to pay most of these disbursements from my teacher's salary, which was boosted by extra income earned from translation assignments. Thus, I was often able to cover many of our costs. At other times, however, there were bills that remained outstanding and I was forced to go into debt for quite a while.

54. Instructors' Remunerations (*by T. Ochiai*)

For the first twelve years or so after the founding of the Kodokan, all rent and other charges for the upkeep of the Kodokan were paid by Kano alone. Later, a small amount was charged to members as a dojo fee, and for a period of ten years a portion of Kano's payments was covered by income from these dojo fees and from members' enrollment fees. Although the reasons why Kano did not charge students for tuition in the early days are mentioned above, I wish to add some further clarification here.

Kano always maintained that it was never his intention to charge fees for instructing his students in judo at the Kodokan. Therefore, still today no fees are charged for actual tuition; however, the modest fees that are charged are used solely to cover the costs of repair work and building maintenance. Kano's main purpose was to teach judo as a way of life. Jesus, Buddha, Confucius, Socrates and others taught their respective 'ways' to their followers in order to help them lead contented lives. Legend has it that these sages spent much time in traveling and sought to help especially those who were in difficulty and those who wished for truth. They attempted to popularize their teachings widely out of an altruistic desire to help others.

Likewise, Kano had no wish to charge his students for instructing them in judo; in fact, remuneration was never a matter of consideration. If, however, one wishes to receive remuneration for the teaching of a subject, then naturally many would be driven by the profit motive and thus seek to do the minimum amount of work, in return for the maximum amount of monetary reward. There would be little thought given to achieving a reasonable balance between one's efforts and remuneration, thus the spirit of altruism would be lost. It is believed by many people that none of the great religious leaders of the past ever gave consideration to remuneration. Although education has little to do with religion, it does nevertheless resemble religion in some respects. Over time, however, Kano's salary proved to be insufficient to support the growing monetary responsibilities of his lifestyle. Without receiving extra income to finance his activities, the continuation of Kano's aim of teaching the 'judo way of life' was not feasible; therefore, in tandem with the continuing expansion of the Kodokan, he needed to obtain not only sporadic, but some source of regular financial assistance.

If the parents of successful students feel that they owe a debt of gratitude to the teacher, they may offer the teacher a handsome reward. In this instance, it is natural that the teacher should accept it. Again, if parents are not too proud to obtain the favors of others, and in return offer them payment, this is understandable from the point of view of the both school administrators and the teachers themselves, to accept reward. In the case of the parent-child relationship, for example, the parent rears the child and after the child has reached adulthood, the parent does not expect to receive any monetary reward from the child. Should the child develop into a fine and able person, no doubt the parents will feel satisfied. Although the child pays no remuneration to his parents, as an adult, he often feels obligated to care for them in their old age. Kano believed that this should be so.

As above mentioned, the early Kodokan judo teachers, similar to the stoics, led ascetic, humble and as a consequence, somewhat uncomfortable lives, but this was not what Kano had intended. An example of the essence of Kano's judo principle *Seiryoku Zenyo* is that man should demonstrate wholehearted efficiency in his work in return for remuneration allowing him to afford and obtain sufficient food, adequate housing, clothing, enough time to enjoy hobbies and thus a measure of contentment in life. Anything in excess of these necessities and requirements, however, is luxury and should be strictly curtailed.

In addition to his comments on education, I recall Kano saying that this same judo principle is applicable to those engaged in all types of commerce. The result of efforts by businessmen, civil servants and others should be manifested by increased efficiency, which as a result, benefits society and the greatest of these benefits to society is reasonableness in the cost of living for the average family man. If this objective be achieved, he maintained, the number of industrial disputes between labor and management would decrease.

55. Creation of Kodokan Judo Katas

The following is a brief account of the circumstances surrounding the formulation of Kodokan judo *katas*. Earlier, I mentioned the situation with regard to jujutsu at the end of the feudal period when I took up the practice of both jujutsu *kata* and *randori*. Before that time, practically all jujutsu training consisted solely of *kata*. Jujutsu *randori* training, based on *kata*, was not widely introduced until after 1867. Jujutsu masters of the day studied methods of performing their techniques in *randori* fashion and lately such training has become popular. Thus, before the start of the Meiji period, in 1868, the vast majority of jujutsu masters did not teach *randori* at all.

When I began learning jujutsu under masters of the Tenjin Shinyo ryu and Kito ryu, however, they taught both *kata* and *randori*. From a rational point of view, this is natural, for jujutsu must never be considered wholly one or the other, but a combination of both.

Learning *kata* is similar to the learning of grammar for the study of writing and *randori* practice is similar to the practice of writing itself. In other words, in order to write a composition, a grasp of grammar is needed. Thus, in order to perform *randori* well, knowledge of *kata* is necessary. And yet, no matter how well one has mastered grammar, it does not presuppose that one can write fine literature. On the other hand, if one knows only a smattering of grammar, one cannot write well at all. This principle is the same as that in jujutsu, if we do not study *kata*, we can still learn methods of attack and defense, yet on the other hand, we cannot hope to master them.

The drawback, however, is that by constantly practicing *kata* only, one would be dumbfounded if one's adversary unexpectedly attacked one with an unfamiliar technique. Therefore, no matter how one was attacked, for both attacker and defender the outcome would be a fight. In light of this, jujutsu practice comprising both *kata* and *randori* was introduced. I therefore decided to carry out studies on both *kata* and *randori*. Although we may gain much experience in *randori*, we are unable to perform *kata*. In addition, the practice of *randori* is more realistic in preparation for an actual encounter and usually of much more interest than the performance of *kata*. Therefore, if students are left to their own discretion, the majority will no doubt practice *randori* and *kata* will be neglected.

In the early days of the Kodokan, I did not teach much *kata*. I decided, however, that when I did give the odd lesson, I would do so during rest breaks from bouts of *randori*. By the same token, I believe that students of literature should not be taught grammar in isolation, but together with practical instruction in the skills of writing. In those days I taught *kata* personally, to each student, but gradually their numbers increased. To give all students individual instruction became a very time-consuming process. I therefore had to ask one of my senior students to replace me in leading the *randori* sessions and I recall that I had difficulties in deciding how best to teach *kata*. It was shortly thereafter that I realized that new judo *katas* were needed.

56. Kata Research

Following the establishment of the Kodokan, I taught my judo students both the traditional Tenjin Shinyo and Kito jujutsu *katas*. Even though both contain some excellent techniques, I was not entirely satisfied with them since I found them to be somewhat lacking in practicality for use in judo. I therefore decided to create a full set of judo *katas*. The first one that I created was *Nage no Kata*. Initially I compiled only ten throws, but later added five more, the major additions being *kata-guruma* and *sumi-otoshi*. I have not made any further changes to it since then; thus, the number of techniques remains the same today, fifteen in total.

I devised these judo *katas* mainly for the purpose of illustrating important points that I wished to explain to my students during breaks in *randori* practice. These are in essence the critical principles of judo, showing how the opponent's balance might be disturbed in certain directions, for instance. When there were many trainees present on the mat, I found it difficult to demonstrate all the *Nage no Kata* techniques. Therefore in an effort to explain these principles, I would choose throws that are representative of each of the five groups, including the three *masutemi* and the three *yokosutemi* throws and compare the way in which the hands, hips or legs play major roles in the correct execution of the throws. By practicing *Nage no Kata*, my students were better able to grasp more quickly how these throwing techniques should be executed for maximum effect in *randori*. Similar in number to *Nage no Kata*, *Katame no Kata* now also comprises fifteen techniques, but originally it too contained only ten. The groundwork techniques are divided into three groups: hold-downs, strangle holds and arm locks. Again, by practicing *Katame no Kata,* students can speedily gain an understanding of how best and in which direction to react in response to the opponent's attempts at escape.

I devised *Kime no Kata* somewhat later. Originally, I had planned to use only fourteen or fifteen techniques. However, its final form became twenty in total, eight performed from the formal *seiza* sitting position, and twelve performed while standing.

By dint of practicing both *Nage no Kata* and *Katame no Kata*, students are able to learn quickly the basic principles of *randori*. *Kime no Kata*, on the other hand, is completely different; it is a combative *kata* and as such is sometimes referred to as *Shinken Shobu no Kata*. Techniques of this type, using wooden imitation weapons, are based on life or death situations, and were often taught at jujutsu schools.

Maybe this is not true in every case, but it has often been said that jujutsu men in former times executed *kata* not as many martial arts practitioners do today rather passively, but with extreme verve and spirit. Some jujutsu *kata* techniques are too dangerous to allow in *randori*. Beginners are therefore taught such skills stage by stage and in slow motion. This teaching method, however, tends to result in students being somewhat less proficient in the execution of the techniques than would be desirable for use on the battlefield. I believe that the principal reasons for the creation and practice of *kata* are still not fully understood by many modern-day judo students and therefore trainees fail to appreciate the true relevance of *kata*. When this is so and they are unable to comprehend the real purpose of a *kata* technique, I feel somewhat disappointed.

57. Judo Katas Sanctioned by the Butokukai

In 1906, when I was finalizing the compilation of *Katame no Kata* and *Kime no Kata*, I received advice and co-operation from a number of jujutsu masters. They were all members of the Dai Nippon Butokukai, which in those days was headed by Viscount Kanetake Oura. Of course, it was quite natural that each particular jujutsu master should wish to promote the practice of his own school's *kata* techniques; nevertheless, the general consensus was that only one set of judo *katas* be standardized by the Dai Nippon Butokukai. After discussions with these teachers and with the able assistance of Hidemi Totsuka of the Totsuka-ha *Yoshin ryu* and Kumon Hoshino of *Shiten ryu*, I devised judo *katas* that were based on jujutsu artistry. These judo *katas* were, upon the approval of a committee of jujutsu masters, finally sanctioned by the Butokukai for use nationwide.

I later created a basic Kodokan *Shobu no Kata*, in which I incorporated several new techniques. The committee of jujutsu teachers, headed by Totsuka, Hoshino and I, finalized the eight seated and twelve standing techniques for *Kime no Kata*. This was, incidentally, the fundamental *kata* from which other Kodokan *katas* were created. Based on newly composed techniques and my own preliminary jujutsu research, I contended that *Kime no Kata* was suitable not only for practice at the Butokukai but also for practice at the Kodokan.

My original *Katame no Kata* was conceived for the Butokukai and it contained ten techniques, but I later added five more and this revised version eventually gained sanction by the Butokukai. I also considered *Katame no Kata* a suitable practice for Kodokan students. Since *Nage no Kata* was passed by the Butokukai committee without any recommendations for changes, it is today in all respects the original Kodokan *Nage no Kata*.

58. Ju no Kata and Go no Kata

Ju no Kata is not a representative *kata* of the Butokukai, but a Kodokan creation, very different from traditional *kata*. It is now, however, practiced not only at the Kodokan but also at the Butokukai and elsewhere. *Ju no Kata* was created around 1887. By performing this *kata*, one can learn much of the theory of judo. For example, one learns to appreciate the essence of the Japanese proverb *Ju yoku go o seisuru* 'the soft and pliable overcomes the hard and powerful.' In the early Kodokan days, when few were practicing judo, I was able to instruct each trainee during *randori* sessions by advising him at a certain point how best to exert power, when to move forward, backward or whatever. Because the number of trainees increased, it soon became an impossible task for me to guide each and every individual. As a result of this lack of personal instruction, I soon noticed that a growing number of students were unknowingly wasting much energy in futile struggling in both *tachiwaza* and in *newaza* situations.

In order to try to remedy this tendency, I decided to give instruction in the theory of non-resistance. If my opponent pushes me, I retreat, if pulled; I do not resist but advance towards him and in so doing nullify his power in order to overcome him and eventually gain advantage over him. Therefore, by having students practice *Ju no Kata*, I was able to show them effective ways to counter the opponent's offensive approaches. In addition, those who for whatever reason regard *randori* as too strenuous, often favor the practice of *Ju no Kata*. This *kata* is suitable for showing students how to defeat opponents and how to move their arms and legs without excessive exertion. By means of *Ju no Kata* practice, such objectives can be achieved. In such manner, rough and tiring practice sessions are avoided and because the opponent is never actually thrown down, *tatami* practice mats are unnecessary; thus, *Ju no Kata* may be performed on a wooden floor or even out of doors. Moreover, the performer does not need to pull strongly on his opponent's sleeve or lapels; therefore, the wearing of a judo suit becomes superfluous. Thus *Ju no Kata* may be practiced while wearing one's ordinary everyday wear, including the wearing of a business suit. When the opponent attempts a strike, one learns how best to try to avoid the blow. Should the opponent make a fist and attack, one must first evade the blow and then guide the attacker's arm in the direction of his attack while at the same time seizing the opportunity to gain full control of his arm and in so doing disturb his balance. In the entirely relaxed manner of a *Ju no Kata* performance, one may learn and practice something of the art of self defense.

There are other benefits that may be derived, too. Not only among judo experts is it widely practiced but also among members of the general public, many of whom say that they gain benefit physically as a result of practicing it. In 1887 I devised only ten *Ju no Kata* techniques, but later added five more making the current total fifteen. In addition to *Ju no Kata* there is *Go no Kata* or *Go-Ju no Kata* as it is referred to sometimes. This is in essence a fight pitching strength versus strength, after which one performer substitutes strength for flexibility in order to gain final victory over his opponent. For a time this *kata* was taught at the Kodokan, but since it contains some techniques that are now considered to be unsatisfactory, it has been dropped. I believe that there needs to be a general revision of this *kata*.

59. Itsutsu no Kata

Another of today's judo *kata* is *Itsutsu no Kata,* the forms of five. Even though this *kata* is not yet finalized, judo people are, nevertheless, already practicing it. The first two of the five throws are similar to techniques contained in *Kito ryu Kata*, the remainder, however, bear no resemblance whatsoever to traditional jujutsu. Originally, martial arts were of necessity both offensive and defensive. In fact, over the years the skilled performance of such techniques has become venerated and is as such now deemed to be much more important than the ultimate objective of ancient jujutsu, which was simply the act of killing one's foe.

To draw a comparison with ancient business practices, before the invention of currencies, trading was conducted by means of barter, goods were exchanged between buyer and seller. Later, a fixed sum of money was paid by the buyer to the seller; this was the first instance of apportioning a monetary value to goods. Early currencies were in the form of rare seashells, and then coinage in gold, silver, copper and iron were introduced. Subsequently, owing to its convenience, printed paper currency, even though virtually worthless in itself, replaced precious metal coinage. Rather than the receipt of paper currency, trust between buyer and seller became regarded as the supreme consideration. Without this basis of mutual trust and the convenience of paper currency, the business of trading could not flourish.

Eventually money came to be valued more than the goods the currency could buy. This change in the basic principle of commerce is also clearly seen in the development of martial arts. The original objective of using jujutsu in an encounter is the same objective as that in *bujutsu*; namely, to kill the enemy quickly by any means at one's disposal, which often included the use of pure brute force. Finesse in the execution of the techniques employed to achieve this aim on the field of battle was, of course, totally out of the question. Often though, the essential elements needed to achieve this end by the attacker are composure, agility as well as technical expertise, not necessarily superior physical strength. Therefore, these elements that are uninfluenced by sheer brawn can indeed determine the outcome in a fight to the death. Such elements have become highly regarded in *bujutsu*. The composure, prowess and so forth freed from the purely physical strength attributes became important considerations. Traditional *Kito ryu, Kyushin ryu* jujutsu and other styles have influenced this very significant development.

For this reason the experienced *kata* teacher, giving instruction in a 'fight to the death' encounter, is not always concentrating his instruction solely on a victorious outcome, since the skillful display of the *kata* itself has in essence become an accomplished art form. Thus, traditional jujutsu *kata* is not only for the purpose of a direct life or death confrontation, but in some respects the performance of the skills is nowadays regarded as an accomplishment. This is noteworthy. The ideal is promoted in martial arts in every sense by the graceful presentation of the *kata* movements and by the co-operation between the attacker and the defender in the practice of the fighting skills, which are in truth now much admired. In the performance of *Itsutsu no Kata,* movements similar to various natural phenomena are represented, such as that of a whirlpool; the movements of heavenly bodies and so forth are demonstrated.

60. The Kodokan Foundation

After its formation in rented rooms at Eishoji temple in 1882, the Kodokan was moved to the following locations: first to premises in Minami Jimbo-cho; then in 1883 to Kami Ni Ban-cho, Kojimachi; to Fujimi-cho in 1886; to Hongo, Masago-cho, in 1889 and then in 1889 back once more to Kami Ni Ban-cho. In 1894, twelve years following its establishment, the first fully purpose-built Kodokan building was constructed at Shimotomisaka-cho, Koishikawa-ku, Tokyo. By 1905, however, extra space was needed. Throughout the Kodokan's twenty-three year history, the number of trainees had swelled greatly, so much so, that I needed to have a growing number of instructors on hand to assist me. In addition, there was increasing demand from independent dojos for Kodokan instructors.

The Kodokan had become in effect the centralized authority for the development of judo throughout Japan. This being so, the administration of the Kodokan was changed from being my personal responsibility to being the function of a corporate body. The Kodokan was in consequence widely recognized as the most suitable organization to carry out this vitally important task of fostering the future progress of judo. As a result, a plan was eventually put forward for the Kodokan to be transformed into a legally incorporated foundation.

Following lengthy discussions among Kodokan officials, a draft constitution was drawn up. Dr. Somei Uzawa, well experienced in jurisprudence, was requested to review it before passing it to Dr. Kenjiro Ume, who also reviewed it before the final draft was officially prepared in 1909 and submitted as below to the governmental authorities for official approval.

61. Constitution of the Kodokan Foundation

1. The aim of this foundation is to provide financial assistance for the propagation of both the physical and spiritual development of the Japanese people by means of judo.
2. The name of this organization is Kodokan Foundation.
3. The registered head office of the Kodokan Foundation is at 114 Banchi, Otsuka, Sakashita-cho, Koishikawa-ku, Tokyo. Other branch offices are to be established as required.
4. The assets of this foundation have been donated by the founder, third parties and augmented by other sources of income.
5. The president of the Kodokan shall be one of the three directors of the Kodokan Foundation.
6. A Benefactors Committee shall elect the president of the Kodokan to supervise the administrative affairs of the foundation for a seven-year term. The Board of Trustees shall elect two other directors, each to serve for a three-year term.
7. The Kodokan Foundation shall appoint two auditors.
8. The Board of Trustees shall elect the said auditors to serve for a three-year term.
9. Twenty trustees shall be appointed.
10. The trustees shall elect, from among the benefactors, candidates to serve as trustees for a six-year term. After the first three years of their initial term have elapsed, ten trustees, determined by lottery, shall face re-election.
11. The benefactors of the foundation shall be comprised of the following:
    1) The founder of the Kodokan.
    2) The founder shall nominate from among the benefactors fifty persons to serve on the Benefactors Committee. When need arises; replacements shall be nominated at a meeting of the said

Benefactors Committee.

    3) The first one hundred persons to donate in excess of *1,000 yen shall be eligible for nomination to the Benefactors Committee. Whenever a vacancy arises, a new candidate shall be nominated to fill the said vacancy.

12. If the Board of Trustees or Benefactors Committee summons the Kodokan president, who is also chairman of the Board of Trustees and chairman of the Benefactors Committee, and he is temporarily unable to discharge his duties, the elder director shall assume chairmanship.

13. Should there be a tied vote at a Board of Trustees or Benefactors Committee meeting; the chairman shall have the casting vote.

14. Assets shall be divided into fixed assets and current assets.

More than half of donated funds must be allocated as fixed assets, however, if funds have been designated in advance for a specific purpose; this condition may be waived.

15. Fixed assets cannot be liquidated for expenditure.

16. Expenditure and management of capital shall be in accordance with resolutions passed by the Board of Trustees.

1. The fiscal year shall coincide with the calendar year.

    1) The president's budget is to be reported to the Board of Trustees before the start of each fiscal year. The amount planned for expenditure shall be decided by the Board of Trustees and a resolution passed to this effect.

    2) Before expenditures can be sanctioned in excess of those budgeted, a resolution must be passed at an extraordinary Board of Trustees meeting. Although in an emergency payments may be made in advance of the board's approval, the approval of the board must be obtained.

18. A director of the foundation shall submit the previous year's general statement of accounts to the Benefactors Committee at the beginning of each fiscal year.

19. Changes to the constitution may be proposed by the president and instigated following a resolution of the Benefactors Committee when over half the benefactors are present and when the approval of more than two thirds of the voting rights is exercised.

20. Should the Kodokan Foundation be disbanded, its assets are to be disposed of in accordance with a resolution passed by the Benefactors

Committee. These assets are to be donated to an organization with the same or similar objectives as those of the Kodokan.

21. Upon the inauguration of the Kodokan Foundation, the founder shall elect directors and auditors.

(To give an indication of the value of the 1,000 yen donations, the average annual salary of an office worker at that time was approximately 600 yen.)

In 1918, the above Constitution of the Kodokan Foundation was amended as follows.

62. Revised Constitution of the Kodokan Foundation

1. The aim of this foundation is to provide financial assistance for the propagation of both the physical and spiritual development of the Japanese people by means of judo.
2. The name of this organization is Kodokan Foundation.
3. The registered head office of the Kodokan Foundation is at 114 Banchi, Otsuka, Sakashita-cho, Koishikawa-ku, Tokyo. Other branch offices are to be established as required.
4. The assets of the foundation have been donated by the founder, third parties and augmented by other sources of income.
5. The president of the Kodokan shall be one of the three directors of the Kodokan Foundation.
6. The Benefactors Committee shall elect the Kodokan president to supervise the administrative affairs of the foundation for a seven-year term. The Board of Trustees shall elect two other directors, each to serve the foundation for a term of three years. All directors shall be eligible for re-election.
7. Should the president of the Kodokan be unable to carry out his duties; a deputy shall be chosen from among the directors.
8. Two auditors shall be appointed to serve the Kodokan Foundation.
9. The Board of Trustees shall elect the said auditors to serve for a three-year term.
10. The trustees serving this foundation shall number between twenty and forty.

11. The trustees shall be elected, within the above-mentioned limit, from among the benefactors and serve until a subsequent election. They shall be eligible for re-election.

    1) If a vacancy occurs or if additional trustees are required, the president, at the request of the Board of Trustees, shall appoint from among the benefactors, replacements or additional candidates to serve as trustees until a subsequent election.

12. Every three years the president shall call a meeting of benefactors in order to elect candidates to the Board of Trustees.

13. The Benefactors Committee shall be comprised of the following. However, the benefactors referred to in article No. 3 below shall be permitted to resign voluntarily.

    1) The founder.

    2) The founder shall nominate up to 100 benefactors, and whenever need arises, he shall appoint replacements.

    3) If the number of people donating over 1,000 yen exceeds 200, the president shall choose the first 200 donors as trustees. Should the number of trustees fall below 200, the president shall nominate new members to fill such vacancies.

14. The president shall assume the post of chairman and be responsible for summoning the Board of Trustees and the Benefactors Committee. In the absence of the president, the elder director shall assume chairmanship.

15. Whenever there is a tied vote at either a meeting of the Board of Trustees or Benefactors Committee, the chairman shall have the casting vote.

16. The assets of the foundation shall be divided into fixed assets and current assets. More than half of the total donations are to be allocated as fixed assets; however, if funds are needed for a specific purpose, this rule may be waived.

17. Fixed assets shall not be liquidated for the purpose of expenditure.

18. The expenditure of funds shall be administered by management in accordance with the by-laws and resolutions passed by the Board of Trustees.

19. The fiscal year shall coincide with the calendar year.

    1) At the end of the previous calendar year, the president of the Board of Trustees shall issue a report on the planned expen-

diture for the succeeding year. The size of the budget shall be decided and passed by a resolution.

2) An extraordinary meeting of trustees shall consult and accept or reject a motion for any non-budgeted item of expenditure or any expenditure in excess of budget.

3) In the event of an emergency, payments may be made in advance of approval by the Board of Trustees; however, the board's approval must be obtained.

20. A statement of accounts listing planned expenditures is to be reported to the Benefactors Committee by a director of the foundation at the beginning of each fiscal year.

21. Changes to the constitution may be proposed by the president and come into effect following passage of a resolution by the Benefactors Committee only when over half the benefactors are present and when there is approval by more than two thirds of the exercised voting rights. Each benefactor shall have the right to vote by written proxy.

1) If a motion is passed to relocate the registered head office address of the Kodokan Foundation, stated in article No. 3 above, the aforementioned article No. 21 shall be waived, and a resolution to that effect shall be passed by the Board of Trustees.

22. Should the Kodokan Foundation be disbanded, its assets are to be disposed of in accordance with a resolution passed by the Benefactors Committee. These assets are to be donated to an organization with the same or similar objectives as this foundation.

23. Any recommended revisions made to this constitution shall be submitted to the relevant ministerial authorities for approval.

Addendum: *The next Board of Trustees' election is to be held on July 3, 1920.*
Dated:June 1918

The first official elected to the Kodokan Foundation was the president, Jigoro Kano. Also elected were two directors, Reijiro Wakatsuki and Eizo Yahagi, a Doctor of Laws. The elected auditors were Viscount Eiichi Shibusawa and Tanizo Kakinuma. Later, there was a reshuffle and Kano's nephew, Tokusaburo Kano, was nominated to replace Eizo Yahagi. Following the death of Kakinuma, Toyoji Wada was elected to this position as auditor and after Wada's death Shintaro Ohashi replaced Wada.
In the wake of the inauguration of the Kodokan Foundation, all efforts

were increasingly directed towards promoting the diffusion of judo. A large and impressive signboard bearing the name 'Kodokan' was erected above the entrance in place of the much smaller one that had long been in use. Despite the fact that we did not advertise for new students, the reputation of the dojo was quickly spread by word of mouth and the number of trainees grew speedily. Even in the earliest days of our founding, it was never my intention to rely on charity. I believed that as far as possible we should be self-reliant, and in such manner, the Kodokan made steady progress.

Before the foundation was established, I sought no donations whatsoever from other quarters. In 1909, however, following announcement of the creation of the Kodokan Foundation, we received a few donations from members of the Kodokan. We did not actively solicit funds from the public at large. I donated 10,000 yen and a number of my associates did likewise. I gave a further 20,000 yen as did others, and the foundation received in total around 200,000 yen in donations. Because of this generous support, the Kodokan prospered for a time and we decided not to make any direct appeal to the public for donations. Later, however, the situation changed. Funds dwindled and as such the main concern of the Kodokan administrators soon became financial. Nevertheless, we strove on against this difficulty and progressed somewhat. Strange as this may seem, this harsh experience eventually became a source of our strength.

63. Nationwide Appeal for Funding

The formation, last year, of the Kodokan Supporters' Club, marked the first time in our forty-year history that we had sought donations on such a wide scale. The amount of money that we received proved to be especially generous considering the fact that the Japanese economy was at that time in recession. Many of those who contributed had little money to spare, but out of admiration for our efforts over the years they gave us their unstinting support. Nonetheless, the underlying strength of the Kodokan membership still remained the same, one based on a spirit of self-reliance and fortitude, a tradition that stretches back to the founding of our institution.

Why did we solicit donations during such a difficult economic period? It was unavoidable. We had no choice. We needed funds urgently in order to expand our facilities, for the countrywide number of judo trainees had increased markedly, especially so at the Kodokan, where total membership had swelled to over 40,000. Of this figure, some 15,000 were of black belt grade. This current year alone the number of newly graded black belt holders throughout Japan has already reached 2,811. The totals for those achieving black belt grade for each of the previous four years have shown an ascending expansion: 757, 1,158, 1,354 and 1,704, respectively. This is an indication that the popularity of judo continues to grow strongly.

Although many of these recently raised black belt holders are registered at the Kodokan; not all of them are actual Kodokan members. Formerly a judo man who wished to gain black belt grade was required to take the Kodokan oath before being accepted as a bona fide Kodokan member. Under today's revised regulations, the Kodokan recognizes those judoka in provincial areas who have taken the oath and proved their skill in official black belt gradings even though they do not hold direct Kodokan membership. Thus, despite many of them receiving tuition from Kodokan instructors at provincial dojos, the vast majority of judo men throughout Japan today are not members of the Kodokan. Nevertheless, once they progress and approach black belt standard, many of them do then make application for membership. Although the number of judo men holding direct Kodokan membership is relatively small, the total number of black belt holders nationwide is now quite large.

Because many more judo men are expected to attain black belt status in future, a figure in the region of 40,000 to 50,000 will soon be surpassed. When judo students are properly trained under a strict regime, they often say that they have no objection to adhering to the martial arts aspect of judo, which has a direct bearing on them physically, intellectually and morally. On the other hand, however, if judo training is not carried out in the proper manner, it could have adverse effects on the character development of the individual.

Since the number of trainees undergoing judo training is now growing at a rapid pace, the need for the reform of judo has become a matter of urgency. If revisions to the training regime are made and they are put to practical use, I believe that judo could become a potent driving force for the further spiritual and physical enhancement of the nation as a whole. However, caution is essential, for if mistakes are made, and judo is not taught in a properly supervised manner it could become an unwelcome influence on future generations. In today's world, we require judo instructors who have a firm knowledge of ethics and learning in other fields, in addition to technical expertise in judo. It is vital that such instructors pass on to their successors the knowledge that they themselves have gained. Also a fund needs to be established to help subsidize the salaries of judo instructors and so provide them with a reasonable standard of living.

In line with the expanding judo population, the time has now come for a comprehensive review of judo. Studies need to be carried out not only on judo but also on *bujutsu*, physical training and on the cultivation of mind and on ways of teaching moral virtue. Specialists in these fields should be assembled in order to carry out their studies and publish their conclusions. For this reason, research facilities are necessary. Researchers could then provide a judo teacher with a treatise in order to help him in his teaching duties. However, if senior judo instructors were to carry out these tasks of research after retirement, at such a late stage, it would be a difficult undertaking for them. Therefore, there seems to be general agreement among Kodokan instructors that they should do their own research while they are still active in teaching. Despite the poor state of the Japanese economy, a supporters' group has finally been established. Because the Kodokan has always maintained a strong spirit of self-reliance, even with this new avenue of support, there is little likelihood of our adopting a spirit of aggressive enterprise.

64. Magazine Publications

From the earliest days of the Kodokan, I often gave lectures in the dojo. I advised students on techniques, the principles of *kata* and the true objective of judo – the way to live one's life both as a judo man and as a responsible member of society. Also, I spoke on a wide range of subjects such as what it means to be a member of the Kodokan, the importance of maintaining high standards of morality, how to succeed in life and so forth. Once customs have been adopted and ingrained by one generation, they tend to be carried on continuously. Thus, I made the advanced students also prepare and in turn give lectures to their juniors.

Because of my heavy commitments though, I often had to travel throughout Japan and on occasions overseas, thus my series of lectures were interrupted, sometimes for quite a while. This state of affairs eventually became a problem. Moreover, the vast majority of students attended lectures infrequently; in fact, very few were present at my series of lectures in their entirety. Those who were able to be there regularly were those students lodging at the

Kodokan and the few members who lived locally. The composition of the attendees changed often since they were members of other dojos and as such visited the Kodokan irregularly. Nonetheless, the higher grades and those skilled enough to practice regularly in the main dojo usually came. In addition, some junior students attended, especially those who were also sometimes obliged to practice in the main dojo with more skilful opponents in order for them to make further progress. Because many of these trainees were members of other Tokyo dojos though, they did not always visit together as a group. Therefore, even though the lectures were given at regular times, some of the students missed whole sections of my discourse. Another problem was that a steady stream of new recruits joined the Kodokan and since they had no knowledge of earlier lectures, it was somewhat difficult for them to follow the main theme of my instruction.

Repeating parts of my lecture for the benefit of the newcomers made it tiresome for those who had come regularly from the outset. This was, perhaps, the biggest problem. Eventually, because of my increasingly busy schedule, it became necessary for senior students to stand in for me and recite more and more of my lectures. In addition, delivering several lectures solely on morality, say, sometimes made it impractical for me to branch out abruptly into a much broader field of subjects. After reviewing the situation over a period of years, it became apparent that what was really needed was the publication of a magazine. Since the majority of my students lived in widely scattered areas, a regularly published magazine was the best solution to help overcome the aforementioned problems.

In 1898, therefore, my associates and I met and decided to launch our first magazine under the title *Kokushi* (patriot). This periodical was focused principally on the promotion of culture and was directed not only at those with an interest in judo but also at young people in general. Some five years later, in 1903, we ceased printing *Kokushi*. We next issued a magazine that again contained articles devoted to cultural pursuits but one that was directed more towards the judo fraternity, since it was centered on all aspects of Kodokan judo. Thanks to these publications, I was able to explain and diffuse my ideas regularly in a continuous, orderly and convenient manner to a wide readership. Later, in December 1915, in a further attempt to promote the cultivation of knowledge among judo students, we announced the formation of the *Judokai*, a society of judo enthusiasts.

65. Purpose of the Judokai

The recent influx into Japanese society of Western culture, institutions and ideology has aroused not only much attention but also much agitation. The intelligentsia worries that because of such influences, which are coupled with economic prosperity, many Japanese are becoming increasingly decadent and therefore efforts are needed to reverse this trend. In this regard, judo training could prove useful. In the past thirty years or so since the founding of the Kodokan, we have seen that judo can have a beneficial effect not only on the morale and physical development of many of our young people but also on the unification of their ideology. Because of Japan's increasing economic expansion, the impact of judo and other aspects of Japanese culture on society are no longer confined to this nation alone but now also extend to far off lands.

Today, there are said to be over one thousand judo instructors teaching nationwide. In a further effort to promote judo, some of them, midway through their own training, have become teachers by profession in order to help satisfy the strong demand for instruction from neighborhood children. It is estimated that over 100,000 people on a national scale wish to learn judo; therefore, because of the growing number of teachers, many of those who desire personal tuition are usually able to receive it. We should, however, make greater efforts to send only qualified instructors to regional dojos nationwide. The formation of a national association dedicated to the diffusion of judo training under the auspices of the Kodokan and the *Judokai* should lead to the establishment of more dojos.

Such aims are most likely to be fulfilled by means of books and magazines, by lectures on judo to study groups, and by the dispatching of instructors to the regions in order to explain the aims of judo and the most suitable methods for attaining the necessary technical skills. The younger generation requires guidance in learning how to live useful and productive lives. They should be made to understand the true principles of judo and use them as a basis for enhancing their knowledge and their general well-being. The members of the *Judokai* must also strive to further their own intellectual development.

In essence, therefore, the *Judokai* needs to be focused on teaching not only the techniques of judo but also on the spiritual aspects. This will help lead to the development of a more responsible citizenry. I believe that the aims of this organization, as a result of compliance with its rules and regulations, will attract a growing number of people to the judo movement.

Jigoro Kano
December 1915

66. Judokai Regulations

1. The name of this society is *Judokai*. Its primary aims are to promote both the development and the diffusion of judo.
2. These objectives shall be pursued by means of the following:
   A. book and magazine publications.
   B. lectures and training courses.
   C. the dispatch of inspectors and instructors to teach and
   D. encourage the diffusion of judo among students.
3. The registered head office of the *Judokai* is at 114 Banchi, Sakashita-machi, Otsuka, Koishikawa-ku, Tokyo. Other branches of the *Judokai* are to be established as required.
4. The *Judokai* membership shall be drawn from those who support the ideals of this society.
5. Those who wish to become members shall pay an entrance fee of 50 sen.
6. Annual membership dues of 150 sen shall be paid in advance. For members who so wish, dues of 150 sen may be paid in three 50-sen installments. Life membership is 20 yen.
7. Members are entitled to receive a complimentary copy of the monthly magazine *Judokai* in addition to the following rights and privileges.
   A. Members may attend *Judokai* lectures and training courses.
   B. Members are entitled to discounts on *Judokai* publications.
   C. Members may seek advice related to judo.
   D. Kodokan membership is open to all *Judokai* members who are non-Tokyo residents, and to those who have been formally introduced and who promise to abide by the Kodokan regulations.
8. Those individuals meeting either of the two following conditions are also eligible for *Judokai* membership.
   A. Candidates who have been recommended by senior *Judokai*

members.

    B. Benefactors who have made donations to either the *Judokai* or to the Kodokan Foundation.

9. A member who pays annual dues of 150 sen in advance may receive the *Judokai* magazine.

10. Each member shall receive a *Judokai* membership card.

11. Members making application may receive a *Judokai* badge.

12. Members who have given meritorious service to the *Judokai* shall be awarded distinguished service certificates.

13. Any member who commits an illegal act shall be removed from the *Judokai* register following a resolution to this effect passed by the Board of Trustees.

14. The *Judokai* administration shall consist of a chairman, ten directors, trustees and committee members.

15. The president of the Kodokan shall appoint the *Judokai* chairman and give him full and complete authority over Judokai affairs.

    A. The chairman shall appoint directors with responsibility for the management of the five departments described in Article 16 below.

    B. The trustees shall select one of their number to be the chairman of the Board of Trustees. Whenever summoned, the thirty permanent trustees shall assist the chairman in revising regulations and drawing up by-laws.

    C. Whenever necessary, the chairman shall appoint counselors to assist the *Judokai* administration in carrying out both central and regional administrative duties.

16. Five departments shall be created to deal with general affairs, accounting, editing, research and education.

17. Whenever there is a tied vote at a Board of Trustees meeting, the chairman shall have the casting vote.

18. Trustees shall serve a three-year term.

19. In the absence of the chairman, a deputy shall be nominated to carry out temporarily the duties of chairman.

20. The fiscal year of the *Judokai* shall coincide with the calendar year.

21. Expenditure shall be administered by management in accordance with the funds budgeted, the by-laws and resolutions passed by the Board of Trustees.

22. In order to revise these regulations, the chairman shall put before the Board of Trustees an amendment, which shall be balloted on.

Addendum
1. Those seeking *Judokai* membership shall submit to the head office an application form duly completed as below, together with the required entrance fee and membership fee.

Format of Application Form:
   To the chairman of the Judokai, Jigoro Kano:

   I hereby apply for membership of the Judokai and promise to obey all rules and regulations of the said Judokai.

   Date

   Full Name

   Address

   Date of Birth

   Name of Company or School

2. Those who fail to pay their dues on time shall not receive a copy of the *Judokai* magazine and their names shall be removed from the register.
3. Those who cancel their membership will not have their entrance fee or membership fee refunded.

67. Judokai Branch Dojo Regulations

1. A *Judokai* branch dojo may be established provided there are more than one hundred members resident in any regional locality and official approval from head office is obtained.
2. Members of regional branches must also be members of the *Judokai* head dojo.
3. The chairman of the *Judokai* head office is required to sanction all officials elected by the branch membership.

4. Branch dojo regulations must be endorsed by the chairman of the *Judokai.*

5. Branch office administration expenses shall be borne by the branch dojo membership.

6. Fifty percent of all entrance fees collected by the branch are to be donated to the *Judokai* head office. The remaining fifty percent shall be designated as branch dojo income.

7. The statement of accounts, showing the half-yearly balance, is to be reported biannually to the *Judokai* head office in the months of January and July.

8. Requests for either instruction or lectures at branch dojos are to be made to the *Judokai* head office.

December 15, 1915

Additional Comments by Mr. Ochiai

Earlier, in October 1898, the Zoshikai issued *Kokushi,* a magazine containing articles aimed at helping young people develop abilities to cope with the challenges of life.

Article 1 stated as follows: The name of this society is Zoshikai. The prime objective of the Zoshikai is to advise and guide youths to help them develop a sound mind and body to meet the challenges of the modern world.

This policy, determined for the purpose of instructing Japanese youth, had three principal aims:

1. to construct a private school for the instruction and supervision of students.

2. to open and maintain a dojo for training in Kodokan judo followed by the gradual introduction of other martial-art related physical training activities.

3. to publish a periodical focused on the aims of the Zoshikai.

The magazine *Kokushi* was the embodiment of these aspirations. Naturally, as chairman of the Zoshikai, Kano was chief of the editorial staff. Over the years, many eminent professors and well-known men of letters contributed essays to *Kokushi.* I recall that when *Kokushi* was launched I had recently qualified as a high school teacher and thought it advisable to subscribe to it.

I in turn recommended *Kokushi* to my students. Later, however, when it was finally withdrawn from circulation, I recall being disappointed that such an informative publication should cease. No other magazine focused on the edification of the younger generation left such a deep impression on me. Recently I re-read some of the *Kokushi* back numbers at the Culture Council office. Even though the essay subject matter is now dated, the essays are, nonetheless, still of value.

68. Launch of the Magazine 'Judo'

The aims of the *Judokai* were firmly targeted on the further development and wider diffusion of judo. The means to try to achieve these important objectives were largely made through the pages of the periodical *Judo*, which was launched in January 1916. I hoped that the magazine would reach a wide circulation; however, since it was the official organ of the *Judokai*, it naturally differed greatly in content from the many popular magazines then on sale to the general public. First, it carried a leading article expressing views on how society should be improved. Every issue contained readers' letters covering a wide range of subjects. Even though I was experiencing a very busy life at that time, both in public and in private, I always set aside time to pen replies to their queries. The following is a brief sampling of the type of contributions that appeared in the early editions of *Judo*.

1] Topics Relating to *Judokai* Activities
   1. Training Body and Mind
   2. Reformation of Society
      A. Ways to Benefit Ourselves and Others
      B. Effective Use of Money
      C. Guarding Against the Excesses of Luxury
   3. I extolled the virtue of exerting the utmost mental and physical effort for worthy causes.
   4. The close relationship between the effective use of one's mental and physical energy and the choice of career.
2] Judo Training and Early Success
3] Judo and the Avoidance of Social Ills
4] Judo and Self-culture

5] Judo and Success in Life

6] Student Life and Judo

7] Social Life and Judo Life

8] Judo and Enjoyment

9] Judo and Socializing

Mr. Ochiai's Comment

The above-mentioned topics were some of Kano's practical teachings based on his experiences of both judo and life.

10] Judo in Summertime

11] Hygiene and Judo

12] Far East Athletic Championships and Judo

13] Mission of Judo and Sports Development

69. Kano's Advice to Judo Students in Training

14] Dignity of the Judoka

15] Advice to Trainees

16] Victory and Defeat

17] Responsibilities to Society

18] Significance of Judo Training

19] Rowdyism and Judo

Mr. Ochiai's Comment

Kano advised trainees to read his articles in order to make them fully aware of the danger and folly of using judo skills for wrongful purposes. For instance, for a number of reasons he advised against their being hired as bodyguards. The messages contained in some of his later articles may perhaps be of help in contributing to the solution of today's industrial disputes involving labor and management.

20] Trainees & Kata Practice

21] The Judoman-Scholar Spirit

22] Tokyo vs. Sendai High School and Kodokan Gradings

Mr. Ochiai's Comment

The aforementioned report No. 22 refers to a judo instructor who was engaged at Sendai High School in northern Japan, and who encouraged his students to focus almost exclusively on improving their groundwork skills during their training. Eventually, his charges became so adept at this aspect of judo that they were able to defeat many of their higher graded rivals representing some of Tokyo's most famous high schools. This led to much criticism of these contestants who overly concentrated on groundwork techniques. In addition, disapproval was leveled at referees' decisions, contest rules and at the Kodokan grading system itself. In his essay response, however, Kano strongly countered all such censure. He pointed out the significance of the Kodokan *kyu* and *dan* grading system, and clarified the complexities of it. He described the qualification requirements for one to become a judo instructor. He also explained why beginners especially should concentrate more on standing techniques rather than on groundwork, and concluded with a clear interpretation of the results of the Tokyo vs. Sendai High Schools judo tournaments. For the above-mentioned reasons, Kano's essay appears to have been aimed chiefly at the judo students directly involved in those controversial high school judo tournaments.

23] Three stages of judo progression: beginner, intermediate and advanced.

Mr. Ochiai's comment

Kano recommended different methods of training for each of the above grades. In the case of the *kyu* grades, he observed that instead of using a bamboo *Shinai*, as is usually the case, a safer alternative is to use an imitation sword made of padded cloth or one made of rubber when teaching children how best to avoid and deal with an assailant armed with a sword.

24] Advanced Judo

Mr. Ochiai's comment

Kano taught his students that the prime objective for a judo man is for him to perfect himself physically, intellectually and morally in order to benefit society. His plan for the creation of the Kodokan Culture Council was one based on these principles.

25] Objectives to Pursue

26] Judo Men's Duties

27] Expectations of the Judo Instructor

28] Pursuit of Lofty Goals

29] Adopting the Jujutsu Spirit

30] Kodokan Grading System

Mr. Ochiai's comment

The above essay titles are some of the contributions that were received from Kano's judo trainees. The readers' column became an appropriate vehicle for disseminating news and for the airing of problems requiring urgent solutions. The following are more examples of the kinds of articles that were carried in *Judo* at that time.

1. Promotion of Emigration
2. For Myself or Society?
3. Rooting out Social Ills
4. Health & Judo
5. Boosting one's Willpower
6. For & Against Adventure

Mr. Ochiai's comments

Kano's advice to the younger generation was based on his past sixty years' experience of life. He stated that one should endeavor to perfect oneself in the first thirty years of life in order to enable one to be of some benefit to society in the latter half of one's life, and that by showing kindness to others one is able to derive benefit to oneself.

70. Essence of Judo

In order to explain the real purpose of judo, a column was devoted to the way one's spirit can be cultivated by means of hard training. These writings were also attempts to detail both *kata* and *randori* and to clarify the concept of what is correct Kodokan judo. Although these efforts helped somewhat in the gradual diffusion of judo practice and were to be welcomed, nevertheless, the propagation of the judo spirit was largely unsuccessful. This was partly because many students performed judo techniques in the wrong manner. It was therefore imperative that they be taught correctly and given a proper understanding of the judo spirit.

Since the essays appearing in this column were intended to inform students of the spirit of Kodokan judo and the right methods of applying the techniques, I myself wrote painstakingly on these subjects. Although I often delivered lectures on such topics, I later requested some of my senior students to take over and to lecture in my stead. Chief among them were those of the highest grade; namely, Yoshitsugu Yamashita, 7th dan, Shuichi Nagaoka, 7th dan and Murakami, 4th dan. Meanwhile, I devoted much of my time to demonstrating *kata,* in particular, *Ju no Kata* and to giving introductory lectures on judo.

The following three sets of writing are representative of the wide range of topics that I chose to write upon for the judo column in those days.

1.   Outline of Judo

What is Judo?
Main Objectives of Training
Attacking and Defending
Throwing Techniques
Ko-soto-gari
Ko-uchi-gari
Tsurikomi-ashi
Hiza-guruma
Dealing with Powerful Opponents
The Point of Attack
Refereeing Rules

71. Ju no Kata

2.

Preface

An outline of the techniques employed.

Set 1

1.		Tsuki-dashi
2.		Kata-oshi
3.		Ryo-te-dori
4.		Kata-mawashi
5.		Ago-oshi

Set 2

1.		Kiri-oroshi
2.		Ryokata-oshi
3.		Naname-uchi
4.		Kata-te-dori
5.		Kata-te-age

Set 3

1.		Obi-tori
2.		Mune-oshi
3.		Tsuki-age
4.		Uchi-oroshi
5.		Ryogan-tsuki

72. Other Columns

3.

In an attempt to make my students more aware of the world at large, I introduced a column that featured reports on both domestic and international affairs. In like manner, an arts column was added covering such subjects as national treasures, poetry, the performing arts, literature, arts and crafts, academic issues and a column that was devoted exclusively to essays dealing with morality. Another column contained bulletins on judo, kendo, swimming and sport-related topics while another concentrated solely on replies to readers' questions.

Therefore, by means of such news reports, essays, readers' opinions and so forth, I endeavored to broaden the appeal of the magazine somewhat while at the same time acquainting the public at large with the art of judo. When free from overseas travel assignments, I spent much time engaged in writing for publication. Thankfully, other contributors, having similar views and experience of education as I, gave me their constant support. As much as I was able, I edited all contributions to the magazine. Unfortunately however, the readership failed to expand by as much as I had initially hoped. Following the launch of *Judo,* around 4,000 *Judokai* members regularly subscribed to it, eventually though the numbers renewing their yearly subscriptions started to decline. Subscriptions from new members did not increase much and despite our best efforts, the circulation failed to revive. In order to cover the costs of printing, monthly sales needed to be around five to six thousand copies. Losses multiplied. Those involved in the publication worked hard trying to popularize the magazine and in the spring of 1923, the magazine's title *Judo* was re-named *Yuko no Katsudo* in a determined attempt to boost flagging sales, nevertheless, this change of name did little to lift the fortunes of the magazine.

Even though articles carried in *Yuko no Katsudo* were pertinent, well researched and a fair number of non-judo people started to subscribe to it, our publication costs were not subsidized by any kind of advertising revenue. Secondly, unlike other magazines, none of our columns had strong appeal to the reading habits of the general public, most of whom favored only light reading. All our articles tended to be of a serious nature, thus there was little to interest the majority of general readers, which I suppose was the main reason that the magazine eventually folded. Thirdly, not all judo students became avid readers. Because of this, the number of judo men purchasing it in the hope that it would help them succeed in judo was not as large as I had anticipated. Fourthly, no doubt, was the narrow-mindedness of my editorial policy, which bore some responsibility for this unfavorable outcome.

Nonetheless, although *Yuko no Katsudo* failed to attract as many readers as we had initially hoped for, it was purchased by a fair number of judo fans and just as importantly, we stimulated among members of the general public an awareness of the real essence of judo. Notwithstanding the fairly small circulation, something of positive value was gained as a result of the creation of this magazine. From an economic standpoint, admittedly there were losses, but from an overall consideration, these were minimal. Despite this setback, we continued our diligent efforts to publicize judo.

73. Confused Ideology and Social Decadence

During my long tenure as principal of the Tokyo Teachers' Training College, I increasingly came to realize the importance of imparting moral education to the young. There is, of course, a variety of knowledge on this subject. We have inherited from former times the accepted standards of morality particular to Japan, which are based on our relationships with immediate family members and with those outside the family circle. These standards, maintained from generation to generation, have been strongly influenced by the traditional wisdom of both Confucianism and Buddhism.

Furthermore, some Japanese have embraced the Christian concept of morality. Japanese theologians have conducted research and published their respective works on questions relevant to morality. In recent years a number of writings originating from foreign sources have also influenced Japanese thought on this important subject. Today though, there is doubt among many as to why and for what purpose we should continue to adhere to certain standards. Previously those in authority instilled such beliefs in the populace, but now these same values are being met with increasing skepticism, and the reasons for accepting such ideology are matters of much debate.

Such being the case, many Japanese have adopted their own ways of thinking on such matters and champion their own theories in defending their beliefs. Among them are some who have little religious faith and merely hold to their own often misguided views. Social development therefore becomes much more complicated as people's desires in this regard multiply. Despite Japan being a relatively small country with few natural resources, the population will nevertheless continue to increase. When unemployment figures start to rise sharply, there will be intense competition among those seeking employment. In former times, a man usually worked all his life in his neighborhood, often because even when employment was available elsewhere, travel to other areas was either difficult or dangerous. He was therefore confined to his neighborhood, and if he did wrong, he was punished by neighborhood authorities and as a result lost his former status. Now, however, if he favors work away from home, modern day systems of transport allow him to travel more freely in order to find work. Should he commit a misdemeanor in one locality, for example, he can sometimes, before being punished, escape to another area to live and work. In such circumstances, some tend to ignore their former moral standards and as a result their self-discipline tends to become lax. For such reasons they are disinclined to maintain former standards of morality that they had earlier considered to be acceptable.

74. Travels following World War 1

In January 1921, I resigned as principal of the Tokyo Teachers' Training College. Shortly thereafter, I left Japan for Europe and the U.S. in order to see first hand what changes the recent hostilities had wrought to their economies and to the religious ideology of Western peoples since my pre-war visits. Although my tour was short, it was enlightening. I completed my research within a year of my return home and confirmed that my preconceived views on the prevailing situation in the West were mostly correct.

75. Benefiting Oneself and Others

This is an English rendition of one of my principles to be observed in life: *jita kyoei.* The difficulties of maintaining social harmony among people do not arise for the hermit. Social interaction for most people, however, exposes them to the possibility that their actions and the views that they express will at times clash with those of others. This can lead to disagreements and to mistrust which often results in disadvantages to both parties. Therefore, in order for one to live peaceably with one's fellows, a relationship fostering mutual help and co-operation is preferable. This means that we should be willing to give consideration to the opinions of others and to show an inclination to compromise. That is to say, we should adopt the practice of bringing benefits not only to ourselves but also to others.

We must not be merely passive citizens, but make efforts to promote this mode of social intercourse and contribute to the advancement of society. One should never oppose this principle. For obvious reasons, a man who chooses to cut himself off from normal interaction with others and live in seclusion usually cannot live a meaningful existence. Therefore, it is in our own best interests that each of us should strive in some way for the betterment of society. In other words, our own moral conduct needs to be exemplary if we are to set an example and so influence others.

Few would oppose moral codes based on such a precept nor would this fact be ignored by adherents of Confucianism, Buddhism or for that matter Christianity. Clerics often expound exemplary moral conduct, which is accepted and respected by the faithful. However, the principles and methods favored by varying religious groups differ somewhat. In the case of education, for example, respect for the Imperial Rescript, which is based on the teachings of only one religious sect, can be misplaced. If one religion is deemed to be favored in the rescript, adherents of other faiths may well choose to ignore it. Nevertheless, the 1890 Imperial Rescript on Education was universally compatible when introduced and has been increasingly accepted by many Japanese people. Largely due to reverence for the emperor, both at home and among Japanese communities abroad, the rescript has become widely favored. In late 1922, I too eventually, supported national recognition of this moral code.

76. Kodokan Culture Council

My research on judo resulted in my deeper understanding of martial arts in general. I mean by this statement, for instance, that in order to achieve any worthwhile goal in life, no matter what it is, there are no half measures, we must be fully prepared to strive body and soul to attain our objectives. This is one of the most important lessons that can be gained from martial arts training.

Basically, traditional martial art techniques are used to attack an enemy or defend oneself from attack in a life or death situation. These objectives may be achieved by a variety of methods. In former times one armed oneself with spears, swords, knives, sticks, clubs or in certain situations one fought barehanded. When armed with a sword, for instance, the objective is to attack or defend by the use of *kenjutsu* or sword fighting techniques. In such a fight, therefore, one must endeavor to use the techniques of swordsmanship to utmost effect. Likewise, one trained in *bojutsu,* must again use every means at one's disposal with the aid of a staff or as the case may be, fight unarmed in order to overcome the enemy.

Until recently, jujutsu was always placed in the same category as the armed martial arts such as *kenjutsu* and *sojutsu.* Those considered to be in a different category were the unarmed methods of fighting. However, jujutsu is, in essence, a combination of all traditional forms of fighting. In many styles of jujutsu, unarmed techniques are used, while in other jujutsu styles conventional and sometimes unconventional weapons are employed. Traditionally the most favored conventional weapons are the long and the short sword or dagger. Therefore, jujutsu should never be considered solely a form of unarmed combat. Whether or not one is armed or unarmed, the ultimate objective in battle is the same; namely, to use all means at one's disposal in attacking or in defending, as the case may be.

In this regard, one of the great principles underlying the spirit of *bujutsu,* the ultimate exertion of the powers of both mind and body as stated above, needs to be applied. However, it must be clearly understood that in the modern world, this principle can, by extension, be directed towards objectives in life quite apart from the purpose of survival. I believe that everyone should try to adopt this principle for positive purposes. The application of the offensive and defensive techniques of judo determine it a martial art. The physical exercise aspect of judo contributes to one's bodily conditioning, the sharpened mental awareness contributes to greater alertness, and the moral aspect contributes to one's understanding of the healthful benefits of adhering to a strict moral discipline. These features can also apply and help to improve one's livelihood by enhancing one's social status. Everyone is to some extent a victim and has to bear the consequences of the ills and corruption of this world. If we neglect to care for our health, for example, in a sickly and physically weakened state, we cannot hope to effectively use our powers of body and soul to benefit ourselves or others in tackling the problems of life. Since our judo training teaches us that hard work reaps the reward of improvement in skills, we should therefore be encouraged by this in daily life and be industrious outside the dojo, too. On the other hand, however, by going to extremes, our health will suffer if we overstrain ourselves by not using our mental and physical powers efficiently. Today, we need to advocate efficient progression. If the basic principles of judo are well understood and if they are applied in all activities, both inside and outside the dojo, one will derive robust health together with mental vigilance and a good moral outlook, qualities which should help one to preserve one's well-being.

There is no better way for a nation to prosper than for the authorities to focus attention on fostering the wholesome development of each citizen. By the clearly defined moral guidance of today, I strongly believe that Japanese society is being improved and the nation revitalized. In light of this, in January 1922 I announced the establishment of the Kodokan Culture Council.

77. Rationale for the Culture Council

Recent world events have made international relations increasingly complicated. If nations fail to reconcile their differences, it will become difficult for them to maintain their independence. Since many in Japan are against such a trend spreading globally, Japan must strive to retain friendly relations with other nations. Reflecting on today's political affairs in Japan, many Japanese have little ambition, their ideology is confused and the moneyed classes tend to be pleasure-seeking. There is continuing discord between landowners and tenant farmers. Further escalation of strife among capitalists and workers could possibly lead to the breakdown of society. There is clearly a growing struggle for equality between the underprivileged and the wealthy. Japanese society needs to be rescued soon from this situation. By adopting foreign doctrines as necessary, the intelligentsia feels a similar compulsion. Those with long experience of research in Kodokan judo have adopted the principle of *seiryoku zenyo* putting one's efforts to good use for the benefit of both oneself and society. By the establishment of the Kodokan Culture Council, this principle can be systematically promoted and make a further worthwhile contribution to the well-being of the public at large.

Jigoro Kano
Chairman
Kodokan Culture Council
1922

Objectives:
The purpose of the Kodokan Culture Council is to promote the idea of *seiryoku saizen katsuyo,* which can be translated as the best practical use of one's energies. This should be applied to all aspects of one's life.
The doctrine of the Culture Council is focused on the following aims:

1. To seek the perfection of each individual, physically, intellectually and morally in order for him to be capable of benefiting society.
2. To esteem the history of Japan and to work to help improve whatever is deemed necessary for the good of the nation.
3. To contribute to the harmonization of society by means of mutual help and mutual compromise between individuals as well as between organizations.
4. To seek the peaceful elimination of racial prejudice worldwide by the promotion of cultural pursuits.

General Principles
1. The perfection of oneself is ultimately the best use of one's energies.
2. The achievement of success in one's endeavors is often dependent on self perfection.
3. The perfection of oneself and society is the basis for global prosperity.

Note:

Whereas the Judokai was largely concerned with research on the technical aspects of judo, the Culture Council's activities were directed more towards the attainment of academic goals. The constitution, however, together with the aims and rules governing the administration of the Culture Council's nationwide network of branches in schools, companies and other organizations, were similar to those governing the activities of the Judokai.

78. House of Peers Nomination

In January 1922, shortly after the aims and regulations governing the Kodokan Culture Council had been published, Mr. Mitsuchi, the chief cabinet secretary, telephoned me to say that Mr. Takahashi, the Prime Minister, had requested that I attend a meeting. During the subsequent discussion, I was informed that since there were few in the House of Peers with experience of educational matters, a number of politicians had proposed that my name be put forward to receive Imperial nomination to the House. I had been totally unaware of any such proposal, so this turn of events came as a complete surprise. Takahashi made it known that he wished me to stand for Imperial nomination. Mitsuchi also mentioned that Takahashi believed that someone with my experience of education would be wasting his time sitting on opposition benches. It therefore only remained for me to choose whether to accept the nomination or not.

My Views on this Proposal

Over forty years had elapsed since my graduation from university, during that time I had held several civil service posts but I had never relied on others to help me secure such positions. Nonetheless, when one is asked to accept an appointment, one should always consider carefully before replying, for if one's heart is not wholly in that particular vocation, one should decline. Actually, I had never had any wish to change my occupation nor had I ever schemed my way into a vacancy. In the past, I had never even considered the idea of becoming a member of the House of Peers. During my days as principal of the Tokyo Teachers' Training College, however, an acquaintance had once asked me whether or not I wished to become a member of the House of Peers. He considered me qualified and asked me if he should recommend me. He said that if a suitable chance presented itself, he would support me, but such a strategy was difficult to accomplish unless there was a campaign to get me elected. Because I had no desire to become a member of the House of Peers at that time, I made no special effort to mount a campaign. The man in question did not pursue the matter further and therefore I did not become a member of the House of Peers while engaged as principal.

This incident made me, however, a little suspicious. The main reason for my lack of enthusiasm in becoming a politician was that too many disputes arise over ideology, and as such, often reach prolonged, time-wasting deadlock. At the same time, I also discerned that many improvements in society were needed. Besides, there is another potent way of bringing about social reforms and that is by means of higher education. In order to accomplish this, good teacher training is a basic requirement. Teachers should not only be knowledgeable but also capable of motivating and inspiring their students to greater efforts. In other words, teachers should also be able educators. However, such people are indeed rare; for few possess such qualities of character. We desperately need institutions where students can be trained to become educators. Despite having as a mainstay the Tokyo Teachers' Training College, little extra funding is available for such an undertaking, nor is the present college administration equal to the task. This being so, the college is unable to achieve its full potential. Although recommendations for improvements were put to past ministers of education, they were not acted upon. I, myself, a lone school principal under the jurisdiction of the Ministry of Education, was unable to achieve my objectives. Therefore, mainly out of a sense of frustration and a strong desire for reform, I finally resolved to become a member of the House of Peers.

When the Special Education Council was formed, I was pleased to be accepted as a member. After I had strongly urged the council to improve the methods of educating teachers, the Tokyo Teachers' Training College was allocated additional funding and in consequence its status was given a significant boost. I had thus achieved my objective in bringing about much needed reform, without any support from the House of Peers, but merely by my being a member of the Special Education Council.

When first made aware that I was likely to be elected to the House of Peers, I was already well settled in my situation at the Tokyo Teachers' Training College. In addition to academic duties, I advocated that the methods of physical and spiritual training that had been devised at the Kodokan be introduced throughout the nation. Likewise, I had decided to launch and promote nationwide the objectives of the Culture Council, which were focused on the attainment of both high moral standards and the intellectual development of the judo man. Therefore, at that time I did not harbor any real ambitions of becoming a member of the House of Peers. Moreover, I thought that even if I did enter the Diet, as an inexperienced assemblyman, I would be unable to achieve much of consequence. For while a novice, and even though I had widened my circle of political associates and gained some support, I did not have enough influence to exert any real sway. Up until the time that I entered the House of Peers, all my efforts had been directed towards the successful development of the Kodokan and the Culture Council.

79. Elected to the House of Peers

As far as I was able, I continued to promote both the Kodokan and the Culture Council. Though it was no longer necessary for me to carry out much of the routine work myself at these institutions, it was nonetheless essential to choose, guide and train those who would take over my responsibilities in the future. This being the case, my main consideration was to instruct and supervise them and since the nation's education system was at last being reformed as a result of government policy, my influence, being an assemblyman, was greatly enhanced.

From this standpoint, the satisfaction of becoming an assemblyman was a consideration, but I myself believed that I had received favor. Therefore, I was glad to have carried out this duty since it was the last wish of Premier Takahashi. For that reason, I purposely did not align myself with political groups when I joined the House of Peers. If one errs in one's judgment, one can easily antagonize political groups and Cabinets for that matter, but by avoiding conflict as much as possible, one aids the workings of government. Because of this, I was satisfied to remain for quite sometime a backbencher; I was thus able to continue putting most of my efforts into furthering the interests of both the Kodokan and the Culture Council.

80. Inauguration of the Kodokan Culture Council

My first task upon establishing the Culture Council was to halt publication of the magazine *Yuko no Katsudo* and to make the necessary preparations for issuing instead the monthly *Ozei* and *Judokai* magazines, which contained mostly technical articles on judo.

The Culture Council was officially inaugurated at 4:30 p.m. on April 3, 1923 at the *Seiyoken* restaurant in Tsukiji, Tokyo. The following dignitaries were in attendance, Prime Minister Takahashi, the Home Secretary Mr. Tokonami, Minister of Education, Mr. Nakahashi, the Governor of Tokyo, Mr. Usami, and Viscount Eiichi Shibusawa. Speeches were given by several of the assembled guests. There was general approval of the objectives of the Culture Council and it was hoped from some quarters that it would contribute to the formation of a more patriotic nation.

That evening, at 7 p.m., a banquet was held at which a congratulatory address was delivered by Kazuyuki Emoto following which three cheers were given for the Emperor. The proceedings were concluded at 10 p.m.

At 1 p.m. on the afternoon of April 8, 1923 at *Seinen Hall* in Mitoshiro-cho, Kanda, Tokyo, a meeting was held at which the speakers delivered the following lectures.

1. Chairman's Opening Remarks by Jigoro Kano
2. Ideology after World War 1 by Yusuke Tsurumi
3. Status & Consciousness of Japanese by Sakio Tsurumi
4. What makes a Man a Man? by Dr. Shigeto Hozumi
5. Culture Council Inauguration by Ichiro Tokutomi
6. Kodokan Culture Council by Dr. Yujiro Miyake

(The lectures by Sakio Tsurumi and that of Dr. Hozumi were later published in the magazine *Ozei*.)

Comment by Mr. Ochiai
Yusuke Tsurumi's lecture, *Ideology after World War 1*, referred to a popular nationalist movement formed at the founding of Czechoslovakia following World War 1. Tsurumi advocated that the Culture Council should adopt a similar nationalistic fervor. Although Tsurumi's suggestion did not seem to raise any objections, I must point out that the Culture Council was not intended to be

in any way an ideological propaganda machine. It was established specifically for the purpose of instructing men to perfect both mind and body. Kano simply wanted his students to develop a strong spirit of tenacity by means of physical training based on the techniques of attack and defense. Mr. Miyake and Mr. Tokutomi, both non-judo men, praised the aims of the Culture Council and thought that membership of the organization would be an interesting experience.

81. Ozei Magazine

I put much effort into the work of editing both the *Ozei* and *Judokai* magazines. Copies of each issue were sent to Crown Prince Hirohito, and since the 1922 visit to Japan of Edward, Prince of Wales, came shortly after the launch of these magazines, a first edition of *Ozei* was presented to Prince Edward, too. Yet despite all the hard work that went into the publishing of these new magazines, they were eventually discontinued largely because of the high printing costs incurred. Since I owned a plot of land, I determined from the very beginning to sell it piece by piece in order to cover any shortfall in meeting such costs. I recall that these events occurred around the time of my sixtieth birthday, and well wishers, aware of the financial difficulties that we were facing, contributed money together with gifts on that particular occasion.

By the time I had reached my sixty-first birthday, many friends and acquaintances from both inside and outside the dojo were giving us occasional financial assistance. Since their donations totaled several tens of thousands of yen, we were most grateful for their generosity. The Kodokan was registered as a non-profit organization and therefore not liable for taxation. I was able to meet my own financial commitments for a time and thanks to these monetary gifts together with income from the land that I owned, I was also able to provide some financial support for the Culture Council.

Nevertheless, before long we found it increasingly difficult to obtain sizable funding on a regular basis. Furthermore, publication costs of the *Ozei* had grown while on the other hand our sales volume had dropped sharply. In an effort to increase circulation, we resorted to advertising *Ozei* in the popular press, but this proved to be costly and the resulting response was poor. It was never my intention to make the magazine appeal to the curiosity of the general public, for it is difficult to run a highly successful magazine by publishing only frank, honest opinion. Finally, it became apparent that if the shortfall from both magazines continued to accumulate, I would soon lose all my savings in trying to cover the debts of the magazine. I therefore decided that instead of publishing two magazines, I would publish just one and this I named, *Judo*.

Basically, the articles that were carried in *Ozei* were focused on the current and on the anticipated future state of the world. The purpose of the magazine was an attempt to counsel students how to succeed in life: by advising them how to deal with people, the notion of nationalism, and also by giving them some understanding of how Japan should deal with the rest of the world. Our contributors endeavored to explain and to clarify matters relating to these core issues.

In addition, I wished to bring to readers' attention scholarly views on such important matters as political ideology, economics and social problems. Another objective was to try to help our subscribers as individuals improve themselves while at the same time explain methods of conciliation in order for them to avoid clashes between individuals as well as organizations. In the inaugural edition, I stated in the foreword the objectives of the Culture Council and defined the underlying principles. The following are some of the articles that appeared in the first issue.

Recent Ideological Agitation by Dr. Kenjiro Fuji
Culture and Femininity by Utako Shimoda
Universal Suffrage by Saburo Shimada
A Critique of New Ideologies by Dr. Tsuichiro Tanaka

There were also contributions from Captain Hidaka, of the Japanese navy, Mr. Komatsu, a diplomat, Dr. Yamauchi on biology, Heisaburo Takashima on psychology, Mr. Otani on physical training, Mr. Ikeda on science, and other essays from a number of eminent professors. Poems and articles on daily life were also included in the monthly 160-page magazine.

The second issue of *Ozei* contained the following articles of which the first two were penned by me.

1. Perfection of Self
2. National Prosperity
3. Significance of Culture

116

4. Swimming and Mountain Climbing
5. Characteristics of Strenuous Effort
6. Food and Health
7. Polite Letter Writing
8. A Call to Mankind
9. A Summary of the Genoa Conference
10. Swimming and Health
11. Improvement in Crop Yields
12. Improving one's Life
13. Ridding Oneself of Prejudices
14. Grass Roots Diplomacy
15. Peace Through Art
16. Who are the Bourgeoisie?
17. Current Anxieties in Education
18. The Jury System
19. Advances in Air Travel

82. Association of Black Belt Holders

Since its foundation over 40 years ago, the Kodokan has attracted an active membership that currently stands at tens of thousands of students who are dispersed throughout Japan and abroad. Until now, there has been little socializing between individuals practicing judo regularly at the Kodokan and those who practice at the many affiliated regional dojos. Unlike a school, there is no such thing as graduation from the Kodokan, once accepted as a member, one remains so for life.

As membership growth has continued to expand over the years, the task of maintaining close and regular contact between individual members became difficult. Although there has been sporadic correspondence between Kodokan staff and members living in the regions, especially by means of the Culture Council magazines, communications were, nevertheless, far from satisfactory. Therefore, a proposal was put forward to establish an organization that would help bring members together and enable them to maintain more familiar relationships. Because of our very large total membership of tens of thousands though, the administration work did not prove to be a simple undertaking.

Ideas were suggested and discussed, finally it was proposed and accepted that an association be set up and be limited to applicants who were bona fide black belt holders, who at that time totaled some 10,000 or so. By limiting membership to this smaller figure, the task of administration would be made that much easier. After much discussion, the idea of forming a Central Black Belt Association at the Kodokan and one or more Black Belt Association branches in each prefecture nationwide was also agreed upon and officially adopted.

The Main Objectives of the Black Belt Association are:
1. To form an association for the purpose of communicating and associating in fellowship with the judo fraternity.
2. To carry out and to publish the results of research on all aspects of judo.
3. To record details of all promotion contests and to revise and maintain a register of all members' grades.

While the Kodokan membership remained fairly small, it was relatively easy to administer such a system, but over time the membership grew sharply, the clerical work involved in registering and especially in updating each student's promotion details became increasingly burdensome. Problems soon occurred and then multiplied. Sometimes members were not always evaluated for promotion in a stringent and consistent manner; also the lengthy time lag in revising the promotion particulars of regional candidates caused especial dissatisfaction. Naturally, if grading examinations were not carried out strictly and if grades were awarded on the recommendation of only one or two instructors, those unworthy of promotion may well be favored, which would naturally invite further criticism of the whole system of grading and bring the reputation of the Kodokan into disrepute. In order to deal with these issues, Black Belt Association grading committees were set up in each prefecture and only those students recommended for promotion by these committees were officially recognized by the Kodokan. In addition, a Black Belt Association research department was established for the purpose of implementing scientific studies on judo.

The Central Kodokan Black Belt Association (by Mr. Ochiai)

In each prefecture one or more Black Belt Association branches were formed under the umbrella of the Central Kodokan Black Belt Association. Kano was elected as the first Chairman. He in turn appointed members to serve on Black Belt Association Committees. Kano also selected officials to supervise the administration of all regional Black Belt Associations. The Black Belt Associations were representative of the standards expected of judo men nationwide and eventually there was exacting uniformity.

In the early formative days, the Central Kodokan Black Belt Association played a consultative role, but gradually the regional Black Belt Associations became more active and influential, finally becoming decision-making bodies themselves. Kano himself directed affairs and initially there were few difficulties. Later, however, when other Black Belt Association members succeeded him to official positions in the regions, problems were encountered. It often happens that there are situations in administrative work that are difficult to deal with alone. Nevertheless, when important decisions had to be taken by the Central Kodokan Black Belt Association, Kano was able to muster the necessary moral and financial support from the many representatives of the regional Black Belt Associations.

83. Kodokan Black Belt Association Regulations

1. The purpose of the Kodokan Black Belt Association is to create a network of branches in order to help promote the diffusion of judo and encourage fellowship among members. All member branches shall be named Kodokan Black Belt Association.
    a. The Black Belt Associations shall be affiliated to the Kodokan Culture Council and shall cooperate as appropriate in pursuit of their mutual objectives.
2. The Kodokan Black Belt Association shall be composed of the following:
    a. black belt holders recognized by the Kodokan.
    b. members of other Black Belt Associations, and members of the Kodokan who have been recommended for membership by their Kodokan instructors.
3. For the purpose of co-coordinating activities, the regional Black

Belt Associations shall liaise with the Central Kodokan Black Belt Association in Tokyo.

a. The rules governing the election of the chairmen and officers of regional Black Belt Associations shall be separate from those regulations governing the election of the chairman of the Central Kodokan Black Belt Association.

4. The chairman of the Kodokan shall also assume chairmanship of the Central Kodokan Black Belt Association.

a. The chairman of each regional Black Belt Association shall be elected by the local membership.

b. Depending on requirements, some members shall be nominated to serve as trustees and others as committee members.

5. Regulations governing each regional Kodokan Black Belt Association shall be implemented following approval by the Central Kodokan Black Belt Association.

6. Each regional Kodokan Black Belt Association shall establish a research division and a division responsible for the recording of the promotion details of each member.

a. The results of all judo research shall be reported to the Central Kodokan Black Belt Association.

b. The promotion record of each member approved by the regional promotion committees shall be submitted to the chairman of the Kodokan.

7. Progress reports on the development of Kodokan judo from each of the regional Kodokan Black Belt Associations shall be submitted to the chairman of the Central Kodokan Black Belt Association.

8. A financial report from each of the regional Kodokan Black Belt Associations is to be submitted annually to the chairman of the Central Kodokan Black Belt Association.

84. Central Kodokan Black Belt Association Regulations

1. These regulations are based on and shall apply in the same manner as the regulations governing the Kodokan Black Belt Association.

2. The registered address of the Central Kodokan Black Belt Association is Kodokan, 114, Otsuka, Sakashita-cho, Koishikawa-ku, Tokyo.

3. The meetings of this organization shall be either regular or extraordinary meetings.
    a. Regular meetings shall be convened annually in July and extraordinary meetings shall be held when need arises.
    b. Two months' advanced notice of the agenda, time and date of regular meetings shall be given.
4. The administration shall be composed of the elected chairman, vice-chairman, secretary and branch representatives of the Black Belt Association.
5. The chairman of the Kodokan shall supervise the activities of the Central Kodokan Black Belt Association.
6. In the absence of the chairman, the vice-chairman shall assume chairmanship.
7. The chairman shall give the secretary necessary instructions.
8. Representatives of the Central Kodokan Black Belt Association shall be elected as follows.
    a. The chairman shall decide the number of regional Kodokan Black Belt Association representatives.
    b. Each regional Kodokan Black Belt Association, in accordance with previously issued instructions, shall elect a qualified representative who shall report regularly to the chairman of the Central Kodokan Black Belt Association.
    c. The representatives shall serve a one-year term and shall participate in the proceedings of the Central Kodokan Black Belt Association.
9. The Central Kodokan Black Belt Association shall encourage :
    a. each area to co-operate, profit and progress in judo.
    b. instructors to lecture on Kodokan judo.
    c. national Kodokan judo competitions.
    d. the staging of Kodokan judo training courses.

All of the aforementioned shall be advertised in the public domain.
10. The administrative expenses for the Black Belt Associations shall be financed as follows.
    a. The Kodokan will bear the costs of equipping dojos, communication and miscellaneous expenditures.
    b. Travel and lodging expenses for Black Belt Association represen-

tatives will be paid for by the Black Belt Association. Expenses for representatives attending extraordinary meetings will be subsidized by the Kodokan.

85. Tokyo Kodokan Black Belt Association Regulations

1. This organization shall be named Tokyo Kodokan Black Belt Association and it shall be structured according to the rulings of the Kodokan Black Belt Association.

2. The Tokyo Kodokan Black Belt Association shall be composed of black belt members of the Kodokan residing within the city of Tokyo and those who have received a recommendation for membership from the Kodokan chairman.

3. The registered address of the Tokyo Kodokan Black Belt Association is: Kodokan, 18, Sakashita-cho, Koishikawa-ku, Tokyo.

4. The officers of the Tokyo Kodokan Black Belt Association shall be: chairman, vice-chairman, secretaries, committee members, researchers and counselors.

5. The chairman of the Tokyo Kodokan Black Belt Association shall not serve concurrently as chairman of the Central Kodokan Black Belt Association.

    a. The chairman shall supervise the activities of the Tokyo Kodokan Black Belt Association.

    b. The chairman of the Tokyo Kodokan Black Belt Association shall appoint one member to be vice-chairman from among three candidates. The vice-chairman's term of office shall be three years.

6. The vice-chairman of the Tokyo Kodokan Black Belt Association shall assist the chairman in carrying out his duties and in the absence of the chairman shall chair meetings.

7. Secretaries shall receive necessary instruction from the chairman.

8. The researchers shall adhere to instructions of the Tokyo Kodokan Black Belt Association Research Department. They shall carry out their duties in accordance with the Kodokan Black Belt Association regulations Article No.6 item b. *The promotion records of members approved by the regional promotion committees shall be submitted to the*

chairman of the Kodokan.

9. The chairman shall appoint one researcher to be manager of the Research Department and another to be assistant manager.

    a. The manager shall supervise the work of the Research Department.

    b. The assistant manager shall, in the absence of the manager, assume the duties of manager.

10. The counselors shall perform their duties in accordance with Article No. 6, item b, of the Kodokan Black Belt Association regulations: *The promotion records of members approved by the regional promotion committees shall be submitted to the chairman of the Kodokan.*

11. The chairman shall appoint one counselor as manager and another as assistant manager.

    a. The manager shall oversee the activities of the counselors.

    b. In the absence of the manager, the assistant manager shall assume the duties of manager.

12. The chairman shall appoint one or two secretaries to the Research Department and one or two secretaries to the Counselor Department to serve as assistants in each respective department.

13. Tokyo Kodokan Black Belt Association meetings shall be both regular and extraordinary.

    1) All Kodokan members are eligible to attend Annual General Meetings of the Tokyo Kodokan Black Belt Association, the New Year Kagamibiraki Ceremony and the spring and autumn Red and White Contests.

    2) At the discretion of the chairman, a non-researcher may be appointed as manager of the Research Department.

    3) At the discretion of the chairman, a non-member may be co-opted to the Counselors Committee.

        a. Regular meetings of the Counselors Committee shall be held following Kodokan judo competitions.

        b. Extraordinary meetings of the Counselors Committee shall be held whenever deemed necessary.

        c. Advance notice shall be given of the time and venue of all meetings.

        d. The Tokyo Kodokan Black Belt Association shall be funded by members' subscriptions. Supplementary funding shall be obtained from the Kodokan and from donations.

86. Black Belt Associations and the Kodokan Culture Council

Though barely seven years have elapsed since the formation of the Black Belt Associations, there are now associations in most prefectures nationwide as well as several in foreign countries. From 1922, branches of the Kodokan Culture Council have been established from the northern islands of Sakhalin and Hokkaido to the southern islands of Okinawa, in addition to overseas branches in Taiwan, Korea and Manchuria. In recent years, therefore, I have been obliged to do much traveling in order to lecture and to explain to members of both organizations the real essence and purpose of judo and the objectives of the Kodokan Culture Council.

Following the creation of the Culture Council, I also decided to publicize nationally the general aims of this institution. In an attempt to achieve this, two methods were employed. In one, detailed and in-depth explanations were delivered to a small number of judo instructors resident in scattered provincial areas. In the other, the bare essentials of my instructions were publicized widely by a larger group of instructors and later during my visits to those particular areas I personally gave more detailed guidance to select smaller numbers of students. Of the two methods employed, however, it is difficult to say which was the more effective.

Since my earliest days in the teaching profession, I have always believed that the most practical strategy to adopt in education is to disseminate knowledge to as wide a group of students as possible. The drawback being, of course, that because of a variety of constraints, this has often been at the expense of more comprehensive, in-depth instruction. Nevertheless, with this policy very much in mind, I established the Kodokan and opened my private school, Kano Juku. Later, I became a teacher at a number of high schools and colleges and for a time I was engaged as a civil servant. If, however, I had concentrated my energies on a limited range of interests, then undoubtedly I would have focused on only two: Kano Juku and the Kodokan. Maybe that is what I should have done, because my most important duty, as a husband and a father, should have been directed almost wholeheartedly to the financial support and care of my immediate family. However, not only did I choose to exert much effort in supervising the development of the Kodokan and Kano Juku but I also was obliged to bear the resulting financial burdens as well. I was on the one hand engaged in my profession as a college lecturer, while on the other, busily involved in these other mostly private activities. Thus, all in all my responsibilities were heavy. During my long tenure as head of the Tokyo Teachers' Training College, my foremost duty was to oversee the education of many of the nation's future school teachers. My graduate students subsequently became appointed as teachers at primary and junior high schools, especially those schools that are affiliated to the college. Naturally, in addition to these and other duties, it became an increasingly difficult task for me to find sufficient time to focus my energies on teaching small groups of advanced judo students. As for the methods of educating judo trainees today, the emphasis is still on the general schooling of a large number of students residing over a wide area. However, it still remains problematic as to the best way to teach judo since there are both inherent merits and demerits involved no matter which method is favored.

Normally, it is considered best for an educator to limit the scope of his teaching to his specialty. For the education of the Kodokan Culture Council members, however, I thought it better to concentrate on a less specialized but wider field of study. If my efforts were not directed at educating small groups of students, they were not very effective. Also, it was difficult for me to make significant progress when I had to delegate so many of my lectures to others who either did not teach in a similar manner or share my enthusiasm for the undertaking. Nonetheless, because my teaching at the Kodokan Culture Council was broadly focused, I gained over the years some very able successors, especially in the provinces. I thus considered this experience to be an example of the best use of my energies.

Naturally, I went many times to some locations and made much effort to give detailed guidance and instruction, but owing to the large number of locations spread throughout the country I was unable to visit all of the Kodokan Culture Council branches and affiliated dojos. For a considerable time I continued with my instruction in regions considered to have the most potential and lectured on the society's merits many times. I am at last satisfied that the Kodokan Culture Council network has now been firmly established nationwide and I have many able students, I therefore have high expectations of them in future.

87. Culture Council – Kodokan Affiliation

The close links between the Kodokan and the Culture Council are evident from the above-mentioned regulations, which govern in a similar manner these two respective bodies. When examining their activities, however, it soon becomes apparent that the sources from whence they originated are quite different. On the one hand, the Kodokan was created initially for the purpose of martial arts research. With the creation of judo, however, not only the physical but also spiritual and intellectual aspects became emphasized in the training of the judo man for daily life. However, if we look back to the origins of judo, the practice of *kata* and the evolution of *randori* resulted because judo differed from traditional jujutsu in that judo techniques are based on the principles of physical exercise for the harmonious development of the trainee's physique. Nevertheless, until we have produced judo instructors who are fully trained and experienced in the physical, technical and intellectual aspects of judo, we shall have to make the best use we can of instructors who at the moment have merely the physical and technical attributes.

As a direct consequence of the gradual elevation in teacher training methods, judo instructors of excellence are expected to emerge in future. Looking at the social conditions in Japan today, there is pressing need for the public to be given both moral guidance and ways must be found of improving the standard of living. It is difficult to achieve the real objectives of judo, which will bring benefits to society, merely by waiting for things to happen or by merely practicing judo in the dojo. These objectives can, however, be more fully realized by following the additional intellectual teachings of the Kodokan Culture Council.

Thus, the Culture Council was created in order to try to help the judo man better his ability to tackle difficulties in life. Members of the Culture Council have said that studies designed to enhance their understanding of the merits of physical exercise and of martial arts for daily life are necessary and should also be encouraged. However, the prime purpose of the Culture Council is to act as an extension of judo training, while at the same time freeing such training from the confines of the conventional dojo, in order for its knowledge to better exert an influence on one's daily life.

If the Kodokan had had adequate financial resources, we would have undertaken the promotion of these Culture Council objectives directly, rather than establish a separate entity for the purpose. For over time, the Kodokan's revenues eventually came to be fully utilized, and there was no surplus cash available to fund any of the intended activities of the Culture Council. Because of the problems resulting from insufficient income, I decided to donate my own money to cover the deficits suffered by the Culture Council. However, this turned out to be far from the simple solution that I had at first envisaged. Nonetheless, although only a few years have elapsed since the council was established, it has had some positive influences already, especially on the educational development of the provincial judo population. Further progress is expected, therefore, I do not think that my efforts have been in vain. Following the recent tie up with the Kodokan Supporters Committee, Culture Council activities are now able to influence all facets of Kodokan judo. Such trends are expected to continue. Because the Culture Council serves the objectives of the Kodokan, judo is proving popular. As mentioned above, Culture Council membership has spread nationwide and many branches are currently operating successfully. The total number of branches now in operation at both primary and junior high schools countrywide has reached ninety-eight.

As a consequence of this growth, regulations governing the work of the various Black Belt Associations have been revised and redrafted. One of the principal changes to the original regulations has been the inclusion of a clause that allows members of the Dai Nippon Butokukai to become affiliated members of the following associations: the Kodokan Black Belt Association, the Central Black Belt Association, and the Tokyo Black Belt Association.

These revisions to the regulations governing the Black Belt Associations were submitted and subsequently approved by the authorities. As a result, the word 'judo' has now become universally accepted to refer to Kodokan judo only, not to jujutsu. Moreover, the term judo black belt holder conveys the same meaning as Kodokan judo black belt holder. Nonetheless, one who did not train at the Kodokan such as those in Taiwan and other places or who had not been graded by the Kodokan grading authorities was for quite a time not recognized by many people as a bona fide Kodokan black belt holder. Customarily, only those black belt holders who trained at the Kodokan were referred to as Kodokan judo black belt holders; and those who lived or trained in the regions were said to be somehow second class judo black belt holders.

Of course, this view was erroneous and those who trained in Kodokan judo at regional dojos under the auspices of the Central Black Belt Association were accepted quite rightly as Kodokan judo students. Nevertheless, this mistaken assumption was widely believed for quite a number of years. Thus, the question arose among students: Should one be graded at the Kodokan or at one's local regional dojo? This was a question many trainees asked and finally it became widely acknowledged that both groups were to be treated equally. On the other hand, those who did not practice Kodokan judo, but who continued to practice traditional jujutsu were regarded as practitioners of a separate discipline. However, if they practiced Kodokan judo even at a jujutsu dojo, they were still considered to be bona fide judo men.

The following changes were introduced to the grading system. Along with the increase in the number of judo trainees there was a corresponding great increase in those men attaining black belt grade. The popularity was a nationwide phenomenon. Despite this, however, the standards of the *kyu* and *dan* grade holders were not uniform throughout the country and this led to dissension. Moreover, there was a call from among some regional Black Belt Association members for consistency. Eventually, Black Belt Associations were pressured to recommend *kyu* and *dan* grades uniformly countrywide. Therefore, the Central Kodokan Black Belt Association carried out a study on the most suitable strategy for the grading of both *kyu* and *dan* grade candidates. Since there had to be standardization, a Central Kodokan Black Belt Association grading committee of some ten members was formed. This committee devised a curriculum for promotions that was accepted and was introduced throughout Japan. Such a small group, however, could not carry out all the necessary research. As a result, a separate research department composed of five sections was set up. The parameters were clearly and prudently defined and the work of each section was carried out. Because this organization was newly established and the members of staff lacked experience, they were not able to deal with matters in a complete and thorough manner. In future, however, as the Kodokan continues to develop, other departments will be established, suitable methods will be expounded, and further improvements are expected.

88. 1928 Overseas Travel Diary

Shortly after the publication of the revised Judo Black Belt Association regulations, I left Tokyo on May 24, 1928 and sailed to Europe. Later that year, before my return on September 27, I had attended, in my capacity as a Japanese upper house parliamentarian, meetings of the Expo Commerce

Committee in Paris, an international ministerial conference in Berlin, meetings of the International Olympic Committee in Holland and viewed the events of the 1928 Amsterdam Olympic Games. Unfortunately, because of my very busy schedule, I had little time to devote to publicizing judo. Nonetheless, a few opportunities unexpectedly arose which allowed me to lecture on some aspects of the art.

Italy

While visiting Paris, I heard talk of an Italian martial arts teacher who was instrumental in furthering the spread of judo in Italy. I therefore made plans to meet him in Italy and while there, a meeting with Italian Premier Benito Mussolini had been arranged for an exchange of views on the problems of refugees. On July 3rd I left Paris and arrived the following day at Rome Railway Station to be greeted by a few Japanese and several Italians. I was then introduced to an elderly Italian man. This gentleman was the president of the Italian Jujutsu Association. He had some twenty years earlier trained at the Kodokan and had returned home to teach martial arts. He had reportedly instructed some 7,000 students at his dojo. I stayed at the Hotel Royal where I delivered a lecture and demonstrated judo. Italian judo trainees also attended and gave a presentation of contest judo. Some days later, I visited the Italian Army Training School where I viewed a sports display and a judo kata performance given by a large number of Italian judoka. Although the standard of judo was not so high, I was rather surprised by the sheer numbers of people who were practicing judo. I was told by the president of the Italian Jujutsu Association that he wished his association to have some form of relationship with the Kodokan. He also said that he should like his judo trainees to receive kyu grade certificates issued by the Kodokan. I informed him that I would be happy to see such a practice implemented. Later, as a result of my visit, direct links between the Kodokan and the Italian judo fraternity were established.

England

After leaving Italy, I journeyed to England to meet again Gunji Koizumi and Yukio Tani, both 3rd dan grade holders. They were living in London and were engaged as judo instructors at the Budokwai judo club to which I paid several visits during my stay. I was pleased to see a larger number of trainees practicing there than during my previous visit some eight years earlier. Moreover, the general level of skill of the members had improved markedly during the interim. I was informed that judo had become increasingly popular among both university students and policemen. The day before I left London, these two groups, together with some contest men, held for my benefit a combined practice session at the Budokwai as a gesture of farewell. In my speech, I mentioned the following as words of encouragement:

'It's said that the English do not like to rush, preferring instead to advance steadily, however, once having gained ground, they never retreat. This view is considered to be a national characteristic. Compared to eight years ago, the level of judo skill among Budokwai members has advanced and progress has definitely been made. Therefore, provided that this trend be maintained, in the near future I expect British judoka to compete favorably with those of other nations, and as such, the true judo spirit will express itself by making a contribution to international harmony and co-operation.'

Germany

Later in Berlin, I was asked to give lectures on judo. I delivered one lecture at the Berlin Police Academy and on that occasion the police superintendent showed me an illustrated book entitled Kano Jujutsu which was being used at the academy as a primary text for the study of jujutsu. I noticed that there was a photograph of me on the cover and that Dr. Baelz had written the foreword, but I had never before seen or even heard of this book. It was not my work; it had been penned by somebody else. It was only later when I explained the origins of judo, the basic principles, techniques and the use of judo principles in the wider sense that my audience of police officers became aware of Kodokan judo. The book that they had been using was no use at all in explaining such important matters.

Mr. Aida and Mr. Kudo, both 5th dan grade holders, accompanied me to Berlin and competed against some of the top local contest men. Since there was a considerable gap in the level of technical skill, they showed the onlookers for the first time the true effectiveness of Kodokan judo. Until that time the German police had been using the aforementioned book and it had seemed to them that it was unnecessary to receive teaching from Japanese judo instructors. However, because they soon realized that their belief was mistaken, they immediately requested instruction from Aida, Kudo and I. Furthermore, the strength of the German character seemed to match the strength of the

German physique for this group of policemen made an earnest request that ties with the Kodokan be established, to which I agreed.

Hungary and Romania

I was informed that judo had recently become very popular in both countries. However, on this occasion my schedule was too heavy to allow me to pay a visit to either country. Mr. Ishiguro, 5th dan, told me that a judo association had been established in Romania and that it was being run efficiently by the following eminent officials: the prince regent had agreed to be president, the chief of police, chairman, and the Japanese consul, honorary chairman. A government decoration was later awarded to Mr. Ishiguro in recognition of his long years of service to the Romanian Judo Association.

America

On this occasion I did not have enough time to visit the United States. Eight years earlier in New York, however, I met a Scottish military officer named Alan Smith who had gained a second dan at the Kodokan. He had put much effort into helping spread judo's appeal by opening and teaching at dojos in New York, Chicago, San Francisco and Seattle.

China

The members of the Black Belt Associations in Peking, Tenshin and Shanghai have recently made great advances in promoting the popularity of judo. In response to their invitation to visit China, I have made preparations to leave Nagasaki for Shanghai on December 5, 1928 for the purpose of teaching judo to both Chinese and to the non-Chinese foreign nationals stationed there.

The Kodokan administrators have almost completed the formation of a supporters' group and are progressing in further efforts to diffuse judo overseas. I was glad to learn of these developments. I very much look forward to Japanese and foreigners working together in a cooperative spirit in order to achieve our ideals for the sake of judo.

JUDO'S INFLUENCE ON JAPANESE SOCIETY
by
Brian N. Watson

It is normally in early childhood that Japanese become aware of judo. For most children, their first glimpse of a judo practice session takes place out of mere curiosity. Generally this is in response to the sound of break falls and other commotion emanating from the open doorway of one of the host of neighborhood dojos spread throughout the nation. Run on a commercial basis, these dojos are usually small; perhaps no more than twenty mats in size, and are commonly referred to as *machi* dojos. The instructor, often an ex-champion, lives on or near the premises and is willing to teach anyone who shows an active interest in the sport. Typically only two practice sessions are held daily, the children's class in late afternoon and the adults' session at night.

Boys and girls, some as young as five or six years old, practice together for perhaps an hour or so. Most of them look upon the occasion as a fun activity, part play and part sport. Although they all have one objective in mind; namely, a wish to learn techniques for throwing an opponent, they are first drilled in the two most important lessons in judo; one, how to fall without injuring themselves and two, how to behave in the dojo. These two precepts, especially the latter, are stressed repeatedly at each session in all well-run dojos in Japan. If the instructor does not preserve a well-disciplined regime in his dojo, not only is it difficult for him to teach, but any misbehavior by his charges could result in one or more suffering injury.

After the children have reached the age of, say 13 or 14, the keen ones either join the adults' evening class or seek out a larger dojo where the competition is tougher and the training more rigorous. The grades of the adult members at *machi* dojos are mostly low, often below first dan, and thus the skill level of the adults tends to remain constant. In the majority of cases, rather than for contest, most adults practice solely for the purpose of recreation. This is a view that the instructor is obliged to respect, since these dojos have to remain profitable in order to survive; thus, the instructor has to be ever mindful to cater to the interests of his members. Many of the adults experienced judo in their school days and practice once or perhaps twice a week merely in an effort to keep fit. Following practice, the instructor and his members will normally head to a local restaurant for a meal and a chat before going home. These *machi* judo club activities play two principal roles, one they act as a stepping stone for children to enter the higher level judo fraternity in later years at high school, and two, as a kind of quasi social club for the local community. It is not unusual, therefore, to see both male and female parents practicing judo together with their small children. Occasionally, parties are held or sometimes the members will go away on group trips, thus, the social functions of *machi* dojos help to some extent in maintaining the morale of neighborhood communities.

The Japanese high school system has two divisions: junior high school, for children aged twelve to fifteen, and senior high school for the fifteen to eighteen year olds. Judo practice is introduced into the state-run national school system at junior high school. However, since it is an elective extra-curricular club activity at this stage, those interested may practice judo only after the completion of their regular daily lessons and upon payment of a nominal monthly fee.

At senior high schools though, some form of budo training, usually judo or kendo for boys and sometimes *naginata* (halberd) or *kyudo* (Japanese archery) for girls is included in the curriculum. All male students at state-run senior high schools and at many privately-run high schools are required to attend weekly fifty-minute classes for a two-year period. Often this is the first real experience of budo training for many students. Some like it, but judging by the fairly high dropout rate upon conclusion these days, many do not. Typically, the heavier boys favor judo, and the lighter ones kendo. Before they make a final choice as to which class to join though, there is the matter of cost to be taken into consideration. A full set of kendo wear can be a little expensive for many family budgets, but such wear and basic equipment may be borrowed by those who, for whatever reason, do not possess either. Unlike a judo suit, which can be easily folded and conveniently carried, kendo equipment is heavier, cumbersome, and at times an inconvenience to carry when traveling with full kit bags on Japan's crowded public transport system. Nonetheless, for much of their initial kendo training, a *shinai* or bamboo-made imitation sword and *kote*, protective gauntlets, are all that are required for high school students.

Rather than from a former champion, most high school students customarily receive weekly budo instruction from their regular sports master. Often he is a generalist who is required to teach all sporting activities at the school. Therefore, he may not have a particularly high grade in either judo or kendo. Nonetheless, since the majority of his students are usually raw beginners, his prime objective is mainly focused on teaching them the basic techniques and on giving them some information on the rules and the history of the art. After the first year of high school budo training has been duly completed, some teachers will allow their charges to choose whether to continue with the judo class for the succeeding year or switch to the kendo class. Likewise, a boy practicing kendo can change to the judo class if he so desires. Of the two sports, judo seems to attract a larger number of students than kendo. Some of the more motivated students typically attain first dan grade and a few perhaps even second dan before graduation from high school. Twice a year, students are required to attend a *gashuku* or training camp, often held for one or two weeks at some rural mountain retreat. Although the training at this camp can sometimes be a tough ordeal, it is deemed necessary in order to prepare them both physically and mentally, particularly so before an important judo or kendo team competition.

Participation in regional high school championship events marks an important milestone in the contest career of judo students. It is customarily at senior high school that they arrive at the crossroads as it were, for it is then that a boy's judo career either starts to develop in earnest or peters out. The decisions that they make at this stage often have strong repercussions on them for the rest of their lives. High school students who have done especially well in such judo tournaments are singled out and targeted by instructors. Students are approached and encouraged to apply for certain universities not only by those coaches from the top university judo and sumo clubs but also from managers of professional sumo stables. This is especially the case if the boy has been a successful heavyweight judo contestant, for some professional sumo wrestlers were formerly judo men in their high school days. One can occasionally see evidence of this in the techniques that they employ in the sumo ring. Variations of *o-uchi-gari* and *uchi-mata* throws for example, are popular with many sumo men.

What tends to happen at high school is that some students take to judo training earnestly and continue with their training, or for some reason, they grow to dislike it and merely go through the motions of the rudimentary training until they have completed the two-year course. There is, however, another important determining factor involved here. If they happen to have some respect for their judo instructor, they are usually inspired and as such tend to train diligently. This seems to be particularly so if their instructor is a well-known former champion. On the other hand, if they have little respect for him or fail to get on well with him for some other reason, they often take a negative attitude toward training. This tendency seems to be prevalent in academic studies as well, whether it is mathematics, history, music or whatever. Rarely does a student do well in a subject if his teacher is unable to motivate him. Furthermore, there are those who have suffered an injury or some kind of bitter experience during training and simply give up and perhaps never do judo again.

Around forty percent of Japanese students reportedly drop judo completely following graduation from high school. There are a number of reasons given by students as to why the dropout rate is so high. The main reasons seem to be that many of them wish to progress to university and complain that they have so much study to do in preparation for entrance examinations that they no longer have sufficient time to devote to training, while others mention that they dislike being under the military-like supervision adopted by instructors and senior students at most judo dojos. This regimentation is a lot more severe at the leading university judo clubs and because the daily training there is almost of a compulsory nature, a coercive mood is usually maintained in the club by the seniors. Some students therefore decline to join the top-ranked university judo clubs for this reason alone. Years ago, the choice of sporting activities for most Japanese students was often limited to a budo discipline or to baseball, however, present-day university judo club administrators have to compete for recruits against the growing popularity of an ever-widening variety of modern-day sporting and fun activities, such as skate boarding, hang gliding, wind surfing, soccer, golf and so forth.

On the other hand, there are those students who have achieved some success in judo at high school and therefore they normally wish to carry on with their training once they enter university. Seven Japanese university judo clubs have the reputation of producing Japan's most successful contest men. These clubs naturally attract famous instructors and the keenest judo trainees. Many of these young men, while still of student age, improve very rapidly. The Japanese universities traditionally represented in top competition by most of these leading exponents are Kokushikan, Tokai, Chuo, Meiji, Nihon, and Toyo, all of which are in the Tokyo area. The one notable exception is Tenri University, which is located in Nara, near Kyoto.

I trained in judo for three years at one of the above-mentioned universities and for a shorter period at another. While in training at both of these two dojos I soon noticed the observance of a strict hierarchy among the Japanese students that lasts throughout their four-year period of training. The elder students customarily assume dictatorial authority over the juniors. Not only is this relationship maintained daily in the dojo but it is also observed outside training hours, since all judo club members ordinarily share the same dormitory facilities. Similar to life in some military barracks, slaps, kicks and the occasional hazing of juniors by one or more seniors are commonly meted out, and from time to time, these assaults result in injury.

Although I never personally witnessed any mistreatment of juniors whenever the judo instructor was present in the dojo, it was when he was absent that the acts of physical abuse inflicted on the juniors were mostly carried out. The bullying rarely had anything to do with judo training as such, but was usually handed out for the most trivial of reasons, at times merely in order to relieve the senior's frustration or as a seemingly effective way of maintaining his dominance over the younger boys. Many, particularly in the West, would perhaps view such gratuitous torment of the juniors as inexcusable. However, rarely in life are situations totally good or totally bad, for the bullying did, sometimes, have positive effects also. For instance, it tended to make the juniors adopt a more serious, alert and disciplined attitude towards their training which in turn made them more effective as judo contestants in competition. For it must be remembered that to attain victory in top contest matches one needs to adopt the killer instinct. Some able judo men are occasionally too relaxed, or for want of a better expression, too kind-hearted to pursue an advantage in contest and so sometimes lose, which is of little help to one's teammates when they are trying to win a major championship. To give an extreme example of how a certain instructor dealt with this problem, he knew one of his contestants was such a man and so he took him to one side shortly before the start of his match and spat in his face, wiped it off and screamed some thing to the effect, 'Now get out there and WIN!' which the young man did, almost immediately after the contest started. Being under such oppression daily can naturally result in the students feeling a sense of resentment and anger. However, provided this pent-up hostility in the juniors is expended in the dojo during training or directed towards an attempt at the successful outcome of some other worthwhile objective, such as their studies, for example, bullying seems to be unofficially condoned and tolerated by university judo club administrators. There is, of course, a delicate balance to be maintained here, for naturally if such physical abuse is overdone or prolonged, the victims suffer not only physically but also psychologically. This is where the judo team captain and especially the judo club instructor himself should assert authority and ensure that the situation in the dojo does not spiral out of control, for occasionally dire consequences resulting from such mistreatment have been reported in the Japanese press. The most serious incidents sometimes occur after a student has expressed a wish to give up training and leave the judo club and in response to his assumed disloyalty to the club, he is given a hazing by one or more of the members.

On the other hand, however, when the juniors themselves become senior students, they tend to adopt the same attitude and treat their juniors in exactly the same harsh manner that they themselves were once treated, so this practice is largely ongoing and ingrained among the leading Japanese contest judo men. This mentality seems to me a little ironic since Kano himself lamented so much on how he suffered from bullying in his schooldays. Perhaps if he were alive today, he would not tolerate such oppression of the juniors or possibly he would devise another more passive yet effective strategy for achieving students' success in top-flight competition. For in his day, you will recall that he guided to success the likes of Shiro Saigo, Tsunejiro Tomita and many others. To give an example of Kano's insight, I recollect that Trevor Pryce Leggett, who in his youth attended lectures in London given by Kano, mentioned the following, and I quote, 'I remember when I heard Kano speak about argument and debate. I was then about seventeen years old, and very energetic. I sometimes used to get excited in an argument, and begin to shout. As I was big and even then fairly strong, sometimes my opponent would become nervous and would stop arguing against me. So I found this quite a good method of winning an argument. At least, I thought it was a good method. But Dr. Kano in his lecture said something like this, "In an argument, you may silence your opponent by pressing an advantage of strength, or of wealth, or of education. But you do not really convince him. Though he is no longer saying anything, in his heart he still keeps to his opinion, the only way to make him change that opinion is to speak quietly and reasonably. When he understands that you are not trying to defeat him, but only to find the truth, he will listen to you and perhaps accept what you tell him." This was quite a surprise to me. But these words, spoken in beautiful English by this cultured Japanese gentleman, had a big effect: my behavior began to change. I realized that my attitude to an argument had been inefficient, because it had brought in something quite unnecessary: namely, a desire to win. To bring in such a thing is against the principle of highest efficiency. Dr. Kano had recommended that we study the application of this principle everywhere in life, and my interest in it was now roused. I did indeed discover it as a sort of efficiency of the heart and mind, and found it in very unexpected places.'

The result of Kano's bitter experiences during his schooldays seemed to have aroused in him a burning desire to excel in jujutsu, which he eventually succeeded in doing, and which later no doubt drove him, or should I say enabled him, to succeed in the many other objectives that he attempted in life. Perhaps that was one of the reasons that encouraged him so much to extol the training of the spirit, especially by means of Kodokan judo. As stated above, the regime of bullying still persists today not only at some of Japan's leading university judo clubs but also for that matter at other top budo-related sports clubs. Nonetheless, provided the safeguards are in place; namely, effective supervision of budo training sessions at the crucial time by a no-nonsense instructor and by his equally strict senior students, no serious harm to the junior members should occur.

Normally, the daily training regime for judo students starts with early morning light physical exercises followed by a stint of roadwork for about thirty minutes or so before breakfast. This is usually led by the team captain, rarely by the judo instructor. Upon completion of their university studies, the students dojo training period begins at three sharp in the afternoon and lasts for at least two hours and was, in my day, most often led not by the judo instructor himself but normally by the team captain or, in his absence, by another of the senior students. The judo instructor, when he did attend, would often arrive late and midway through the training session would on rare occasions give a few minutes' general technical advice often in an offhand manner. I must admit that I was rather surprised by how little teaching was given by the judo instructor. Thus, rather than receiving technical instruction, all of our daily activities were totally focused on strenuous stamina training. Typically the first hour was prolonged *randori* practice followed by thirty minutes of ground work, with a change of partner every five minutes or so. The final thirty minutes were devoted to push-ups numbering 200 repetitions and some 300 sit-up repetitions. These were followed by other equally punishing exercises, all done to the count that was yelled out by the team captain who would strike any slackers with his *shinai,* bamboo sword, in order to encourage further exertion. Although some judo students augment their workouts with weight training, such training is not as popular in Japan as it is in the West. Kano himself was not in favor of indulgence in weight training. He maintained that weight training often results in one becoming muscle-bound and as such one loses flexibility and speed and so it can be counterproductive for the contest man. In general, the standard of skill and stamina of the keen first-year university students is reasonably high since most have already attained first or perhaps even second dan at high school before entering the top university judo clubs. Are the above methods the best to employ in the training of judo contest men? Perhaps so, for after two or three years of the above-mentioned daily intensive training, the students become superbly fit and possess incredible stamina, so much so that many are capable of competing at world-class level and some, while still students, have achieved major gold medal successes at the World Judo Championships and at the Olympic Games. Nevertheless, most do not enter judo grading contests regularly and so often their level of skill is not always reflected in their judo grades. Rather than monthly, many enter the Kodokan grading contests only once or twice a year and are, therefore, on average one grade below their true worth.

Because the administration of judo is so well and comprehensively organized throughout Japan, one may continue with one's judo training after embarking on a business career. Unlike the set up of judo facilities in some countries, there are many publicly-run and privately-owned dojos that allow the practice of judo for corporate employees long after their graduation from high school or university. Countless corporations, particularly those in the steel, insurance, chemical and car manufacturing sectors maintain well-equipped judo club facilities for the exclusive use of their staff members. The annual regional and national corporate judo team championships are often well sponsored and given wide press coverage. Although the standard of judo displayed by the majority of these competing players is not as high as that of university students or police officers, nonetheless, some corporate employees also compete as individuals in major national competitions such as the top ranked All Japan Judo Championship. If a corporate employee or corporate team happen to win a judo title, not only does the company benefit from the resulting media attention that it receives but also the status of the individual and that of the winning team members is greatly enhanced within the company. This recognition accorded members of a successful team is a contributing factor in their future promotion prospects, for the team members' efforts are considered to be true reflections of their dedication and loyalty to the success and good fortune of the company.

The Japanese police authorities maintain both judo and kendo dojos at police stations nationwide. Similar to the custom adopted at the nation's high schools, all male police officers may choose to practice either kendo or judo, whereas many of the female officers these days prefer training in aikido. The main purpose of their one hour mid-morning training session is twofold; first, to receive instruction in effective *taihojutsu* or arresting techniques, which are practiced periodically, and secondly, to stay in reasonably good physical condition by means of this regular training. One of the most practical ways to achieve both objectives is to have officers train daily, for unlike policemen in some countries; one rarely sees an unfit, overweight or obese Japanese police man. Of course, officers could maintain fitness by playing team games or by practicing some other sport. However, such activities would not be as practical for them in their everyday duties as the development of the skills, self-confidence building measures and perhaps more importantly physical stamina that results from their daily stint of budo training. I recall that when I used to visit the head police judo training center, the practice sessions were not as intensive as those at the top university judo clubs. Another difference was that many of the police officers were heavyweights and their training was perhaps more biased towards ground work rather than *randori*. Nevertheless, some of the leading police contest men often reach the final stages of major national competitions such as the open weight All Japan Judo Championship.

By and large, the Japanese tend to be a sports-loving people. When a new sport is introduced into Japan, it is not long before an association is set up and clubs are formed in order to help promote it. Although soccer is not new to Japan, it is only since the 1990's that there has been phenomenal growth in its popularity. Wind surfing, hang-gliding and more recently the winter sports of snowboarding, and following the gold medal success of Shizuka

Arakawa in the 2006 Turin Winter Olympic Games, figure skating also has received quite a boost in public acclaim. These sports continue to attract vast numbers of enthusiasts, particularly teenagers. Moreover, very rarely are there incidents of hooliganism among spectators, cheating or of drug abuse involving Japanese athletes. Thus, the reputations of those engaged in both amateur and professional sporting activities tend to be rated highly in the Japanese public's esteem.

In the Victorian era (1837-1901), British school children were encouraged to engage in sports, more especially team games. These activities were seen as a means for children to gain fitness, develop self-confidence, and as a way of encouraging teamwork. The fostering of harmonious relationships with others would, it was hoped, aid society in the long run by also leading to the sound character development of the mature adult. In the decades following the Meiji restoration of 1868, when Japan was intent on rapid modernization, it too followed suit and sports such as gymnastics, tennis and the first popular team game in Japan, baseball, which had been recently introduced from the U.S.A., quickly won favor. However, many of the sporting activities engaged in by individuals at that time were the martial disciplines and were as such almost totally amateur pursuits. Few sportsmen of the day were paid for their participation in games or sports events. In fact, professionalism was looked upon in disdain and was very much discouraged. No professional sportsmen, who by extension included Japan's sturdy rickshaw runners of the period, were allowed to participate in the early Olympic Games marathon events, for instance.

Since the latter half of the 20th century, particularly following the advent of televised sport, the situation, initially in the West, changed quite dramatically. Sports for the first time could be quite clearly divided into two groups: spectator sports, which are mostly professional and which include soccer, boxing and wrestling, for example, and the less glamorous, amateur participant sports, which are, nevertheless, perhaps more beneficial for maintaining the general good health of the nation, such as swimming, gymnastics, jogging and, of course, judo. Similarly too in Japan, the professional spectator sports of sumo, baseball and wrestling for instance, became extremely popular following the introduction of televised matches. Few of the tens of millions of Japanese TV viewers who have an interest in such professional sports, however, actually play them. Nowadays, more and more sports are in effect big business; this is chiefly so for those activities having the most TV viewer entertainment appeal.

Thus, apart from the significance of their value in product endorsement by corporate sponsors, do the millions of fans actually derive any personal benefit from being merely passive spectators of such sports? This is a debatable point.

Because of the huge amounts of money at stake, some involved in certain sports have earned disreputable reputations for engaging in corrupt activities, particularly those associated with gambling. This is indeed a sad reflection on some modern-day professional athletes since such activities can naturally have a less than wholesome influence on the conduct of the younger generation, many of whom are often fascinated by the press-reported exploits of their favorite sports stars.

The situation in Japan, however, especially with regard to judo, is somewhat different. Incidents of wrongdoing involving Japanese judo men and women are indeed rare. Because judo is largely amateur and very much a participant sport, anyone who shows up at a judo club in Japan hoping just to sit, watch and be entertained is likely to be disappointed, for often he is expected to step onto the mat and join in the practice or leave. As with most participant sports, the more effort that one puts into the activity, the more reward one gets out of it. The physical benefits derived from regular judo training can help participants to keep fit, alert and remain active, often well into middle age and sometimes beyond. Thus, judo enjoys a largely unblemished reputation in present-day Japan.

Sports attract people from all walks of life, both male and, of course, in this day and age, more increasingly female. The spectacle and feats of Japan's world champion female wrestlers and her weightlifters no longer raise eyebrows. This is especially so in judo too, for many of Japan's female world and Olympic champions have in recent years become ever more skilled, and in fact there is little to choose between the judo expertise of males and females these days. Some sports are costly and tend to be elitist, yachting, polo, and golf are prime examples. When considering the expense normally required for participation in these activities, such as the equipment required, sporting wear, club fees and traveling expenses, the expenditures can be quite high, particularly so for young wage earners. Judo, on the other hand, is perhaps one of the least expensive sports that one can engage in; this is especially so in Japan. Judo suits are relatively inexpensive and hard wearing. Compared to the fees charged by fitness centers and sports clubs, judo club fees are normally surprisingly low.

Some contact sports are notorious for mishaps and for the resulting injuries caused to participants, soccer, rugby and wrestling, for instance. Considering the great numbers of people who practice judo regularly, serious accidents are comparatively rare. Nonetheless, finger injuries are becoming a problem, particularly so for modern-day competitive judo players. This is no doubt on account of new rules that have been introduced to try to speed up the outcome of contests for the entertainment of the TV viewing audience, rather than in response to any appeal for rule changes coming from the judo competitors themselves.

Among those who take up the sport of judo and train not only in Japan but also elsewhere, I would say that in the majority of cases such people tend to be serious-minded individuals. Basically, one needs to be an active person, quite fit and fairly strong in order to make much progress in judo. Moreover, it takes a little courage and dedication to engage in the required training in competitive contact sports such as judo, for if one makes a mistake or fails to pay sufficient attention during a match, the repercussions can be unpleasant and may result in a heavy fall. Most other sports, however, are much less psychologically and physically demanding. An error or lack of concentration by the tennis player or the golfer, for instance, results in the shot going wide of the mark, but neither player experiences any trepidation during the game or physical pain for their errors of judgment or inattention. However, if the boxer loses a bout he may suffer both pain and injury, but normally not so for the loser of a swimming event, running or cycling race. On the other hand, the judo contestant, similar to the boxer, has to be constantly alert, attentive and in order to avoid being overwhelmed, he has to be willing to fight back and hold his ground, so too in life, in business for instance there is at times intense competition, and often one needs to maintain a robust, competitive spirit in order to stay the course.

By and large, judo has preserved a favorable reputation in Japan ever since the early days of the Kodokan and as evidenced by the huge proliferation in the nationwide network of clubs and judo organizations, it was and continues to be well supported and promoted by both national and regional government and by educational authorities alike. This is mirrored these days to some extent in other countries too, however unlike Japan, there appears to be much less regular financial support given to the promotion of judo in many other countries. Such support is often sporadic. Prior to the holding of the Olympic Games, for instance, some government money may be made available to competing judo associations around the world, but this source of funding soon dries up once the games are over.

Because judo is normally practiced under the norms of the Japanese code of manners and customs, certain courtesies are customarily expected at most clubs. A Japanese business colleague of mine once remarked that he had taken his daughter, Mariko, to the Kodokan to learn judo. I asked him how old she was; his reply surprised me somewhat when he answered, 'Five years old'. He added that he was not particularly interested whether she became good at judo or not. He said that he had made her attend lessons simply to learn good manners! In the West, few fathers would even consider taking their young daughters to any kind of sports gym for such a reason. This, I think, gives an indication of the difference in customs and attitudes between budo in Japan and sport in the West. Moreover, the tradition of judo enthusiasts worldwide observing Japanese etiquette when sitting on the mat Japanese style and bowing to each other during their daily judo training stems largely from the respect accorded to Kano, his teachings and his lingering influence on the sport.

Turning now to the top-class contestant, if one were intent on trying to become a world or Olympic champion at say, wrestling or boxing, one would have to train with and compete against the world's leading contenders. Most of them customarily work out at gymnasiums in downtown city areas spread around the globe. In the case of judo, however, the situation is somewhat different, for the vast majority of all past and present world and Olympic champions are natives of one country – Japan; and moreover, they are almost exclusively university students. Therefore, for a young Japanese judo hopeful, he would first need to become a university student just in order for him to be able to compete against and to train with the world's most skilled exponents. This phenomenon is possibly unique to Japanese sporting culture and is no doubt again the result of Kano's strong insistence, since the earliest days of the Kodokan, on fostering and maintaining the judoman-scholar tradition.

In most other cultures, sport and the arts are quite separate. In the West, for example, a musician, artist or poet would be unlikely to engage in sports such as boxing or martial arts. Not so in Japan. Kano sought to combine judo with education in an attempt to nurture a judo man mentally balanced and with a well-rounded character. His attempt was to harmoniously link the two together so that the one complemented the other. One of the reasons for his creating judo seems to have been the belief that some things of importance in life are difficult or perhaps impossible to teach merely by the written word in book learning. As a teacher, or sports instructor, how do you inspire a student to be courageous, respectful, disciplined, self-confident or bolster his willpower, for example? Not always easy objectives to achieve for most of those engaged in the teaching profession. Kano was of the opinion that one of the best ways to try to achieve such objectives was to have his students imbued with such traits of character by means of their judo training experiences.

A facet of judo not often publicized is that unlike other combative sports, it can be practiced by a large number of those who are disabled. It is seen as a valuable method of restoring self-confidence, very often following some kind of accident in which the victim has been left partly incapacitated. For example, I have, on occasion, seen one-armed as well as blind and partially-sighted judo men engage in *randori* practice sessions at the Kodokan. They are guided to the mat by their instructors and sometimes take part not only in the general practice sessions but also in competitions. Quite a number of Japanese disabled people have achieved black belt rankings, some after defeating not only fellow disabled but also able-bodied opponents. I recall, many years ago there was a Japanese student who was a member of his university judo team. He was also advancing in his studies. Unfortunately, he was involved in an accident and as a result lost an arm. Following this misfortune, he suffered bouts of depression and gave up all interest not only in judo but also in his academic studies. After several months, his mother had become increasingly worried and, unbeknown to her son, sought advice from the university judo club instructor. Their discussion resulted in the instructor suggesting that they should both try to encourage her son to return to judo club training sessions. The judo instructor, sometime later, called on the student unannounced and mentioned to him during the course of the conversation that he should consider returning to the judo club to continue with his training. At first the young man was reluctant to do so, but after a few weeks had passed, he turned up at the club one day. He resumed general judo practice and also took private judo lessons in order to seek ways of overcoming his disability and moreover, later re-commenced his studies. Perhaps the most surprising sequel to this affair, however, was that some three years later, largely thanks to his taking private judo lessons in total secrecy, he had developed techniques that enabled him to defeat his able-bodied opponents and won a student judo competition.

Regular overseas youth exchange programs involving Japanese high school, university and private judo club teams have become increasingly numerous in recent years. Such friendly intercultural activities at the grass roots level can have a very positive effect in helping to break down the barriers of language and culture, especially so among young people. Many Japanese judo students have been inspired to study foreign languages as a result of such experiences widening their horizons. Similarly, some of the Japanese language interpreters and translators active in Britain, particularly in the 1970s and 1980s, were young British judo men who had returned from Japan after attaining 4th dan grade and completing Japanese language studies. A few later progressed further to become university professors of Classical Japanese.

Kano often mentioned in his writings that as a result of judo training, his students could benefit by becoming more determined and persevering in character. He believed that if a student had motivation and a certain amount of fortitude cultivated by judo training, he should be able to channel that enlivened spirit into other fields of endeavor, be that business activities, the study of mathematics, music or for that matter any other objective he wished to accomplish. Another benefit, for teachers that is, which is sometimes overlooked, is that teaching strongly motivated students makes the teacher's task that much easier; for once the student is truly stimulated, he will for the most part teach himself.

Kano also believed that even the most gutless of boys will put up something of a fight if his life is in danger or if he is encountering extreme discomfort or embarrassment. In one's judo training there are many times that one encounters unpleasant experiences and has to fight back in order to seek relief by attempting an escape from a stressful situation, say an arm lock or perhaps a strangulation technique. Kano maintained that as a direct consequence of such experiences, one can in due course become a more determined individual. I would not dispute Kano's assumption in the case of some beginners. Nevertheless, judging by my personal observations of judo men, both Japanese and non-Japanese, I believe that the vast majority of the more successful players often have a partially developed spirit of perseverance before they even start judo; thus their training, rather than instigating, usually tends to boost further their willpower. Such men and for that matter women too typically continue their training long term and sometimes become successful not only in judo but often in other challenges that they attempt to overcome in life.

Of course, as Kano so rightly indicated, a beginner in judo may initially have very little willpower, but if he can be somehow persuaded to continue with his training, and this seems to be the crux of the matter, he will certainly strengthen his resolve somewhat. No doubt Kano made this claim as a result of personal, long-term and sometimes bitter experiences at the hands of senior student bullies during his schooldays. Perhaps this strengthened resolve results also because of peer pressure and the strong emphasis placed on exhaustive bouts of *uchikomi* or repetition practice in judo so essentially necessary in the learning of each new throwing technique. A contestant needs to repeat the movement of the throw literally thousands of times before he can ever hope to gain anything like the fluency and proficiency required for it to be effective in competition.

Kano became a leading figure in public life and attracted a large and faithful following. Many of Japan's present-day professionals, including lawyers, professors, businessmen, politicians, doctors and so forth are judo men of high black belt grade. It would seem therefore that among his many followers, Kano's authority and teaching methods have to some extent continued to pay dividends to Japanese society over the years since his death, for the general educational standards of Japan today are much higher than they once were.

In the final analysis, Kodokan judo, principally owing to its largely favorable reputation, has had, and continues to have, a positive and beneficial effect on Japanese society. Judo's attributes have helped encourage many thousands of Japanese students to take an interest in and to adopt habits of good physical conditioning, a healthy lifestyle, and if the tenets of Kano's doctrine are followed, his recommended 'way of life' is one focused more on attaining contentment and peace of mind in return for contributing something positive to society rather than on the gathering of material riches. Therefore, the Kodokan can perhaps take some credit indirectly for the advances that the Japanese people have made over the past hundred and fifty years, from a developing nation of the 1860s to the world's second leading economic power of today. This transformation is the more striking when one takes into account the fact that Japan, unlike the world's other leading economies, lacks an abundance of any valuable natural resource. Japan's only asset therefore, seems to be its workforce, for it has been said that a spirit of tenacity tends to permeate the general character of large numbers of Japanese. Thus, even when they engage in non-budo sports or in business enterprise or organizational group activities, one can often detect the underlying budo spirit driving and motivating them. Some would no doubt argue that other sports can produce a similar spirit of resolve. This assertion may be true, but whereas Kano's judo is meant to be focused on the pursuit of physical, mental and moral self-perfection, few if any western sports are similarly directed to such high ideals. In the West, many sporting activities are almost totally focused on only the physical development of the athlete.

Despite the many social changes that have affected both lifestyle and sport over the past century or so, judo has steadily continued to increase its popularity in the sports world ever since the days of Kano. Provided judo is not changed into a largely professional sport, where money can sometimes have a corrupting influence on both players and officials alike, judo's reputation, particularly so in Japan, is unlikely to diminish, for the successes achieved by Japanese contestants in the World Judo Championships and more especially in the Olympic Games judo events afford the Japanese public a certain amount of pride. In the recent past, Japan's many judo stars, such as former Olympic champions, Yasuhiro Yamashita and Ryoko Tani, in particular, have been and continue to be looked upon as suitable role models for the rising generation, as was Jigoro Kano in his day. This, therefore, is perhaps the most essential duty for a judo celebrity, to act as a mentor and to inspire one's followers to greater efforts not only in judo but also in life.

Turning now to Kano's objectives, what chiefly influenced him when he considered changing ancient jujutsu into a positive activity for the modern age, and more especially, an activity that he believed would help stimulate a person intellectually and improve him morally? To try to give answers, we first need to look at Japan's position in the world of the late 19th century. It must be remembered, of course, that in Kano's day, Japan had not long since emerged from some 260 years of self-imposed isolation. During that time, Japan had fallen well behind other nations, particularly those of the West, in practically all fields of scientific endeavor. So much so that Japanese leaders of the Meiji period (1868-1912) were at pains to persuade their compatriots to study western learning in order to speed up the process of modernization. The important technological advances in the West, largely unknown in Japan at that time, had led to the Industrial Revolution, which had heralded steam power applied to various kinds of machinery, railway vehicles and ships. This was manifested not only in the great economic surge of the West but also in the possibility of a military threat that this imposed upon other less technically developed nations, which of course included Japan. Apart from these influences on Kano's reasoning, another influence probably came from one of his former headmasters, Shosaku Hida. Even though Kano's maternal forebears had been engaged for many years in the business of sake brewing and his father also heavily involved in business, Kano did not choose to follow in their footsteps by becoming a businessman himself, but instead favored the career of an academic. One possible reason for this unusual turn of events stems from the time he spent, around the impressionable age of fourteen to fifteen, when he lodged at the Hida household. It must be remembered that Kano's former classmate, Kumazo Tsuboi, also lodged with the Hida family at the same time and he too became an educator, eventually heading Bunka University as its president. Could it be then that Hida was somehow influential in giving direction or guidance to both in the choice of future careers?

In their earnest quest for advancement, Japan's scholars of the period translated into Japanese a wide range of specialist foreign language books. Among the most popular English language originals on social and political studies in 19th century Japan were the writings of the philosophers Herbert Spencer and John Stuart Mill, especially *On Liberty* (1859), and the books of Samuel Smiles. Smiles's *Life of George Stephenson* (1857) the railway engineer, *Self-Help* (1859), *Character* (1871), *Thrift* (1875), and *Duty* (1880) were his most important works. But it was *Self-Help* in particular that caught the public's imagination and so became a huge bestseller. In fact, *Self-Help* was translated into a number of foreign languages, including Dutch, French, German, Danish, Italian, Czech, Croatian, Arabic, Turkish and into Japanese in 1871, and rapidly sold over one million copies in Japan. This was somewhat surprising considering the prevalence of illiteracy was still fairly high in those days. Perhaps more strikingly though, was the fact that the Japanese-language version of *Self-Help* (*Jijoron*) remained required reading for Japanese university students throughout the early half of the 20th century, and still, for that matter, remains on sale today. Briefly, the book promotes the work ethic and since Smiles realized that of all forms of encouragement, there is little better than the example of others, he collected a series of brief accounts of endeavor in many spheres of entrepreneurial activity, and lined it with a wise, profound and memorable commentary. The purpose of *Self-Help*, stated Samuel Smiles in his *Autobiography* that was published in 1905, 'was to illustrate and enforce the power of George Stephenson's great word – PERSEVERANCE.' The book *Self-Help* is indeed deeply inspiring and because the Japanese-language version proved so popular in Japan throughout Kano's lifetime, I have little doubt that Kano, being such a zealous educator, was aware of this famous book and may have been influenced by it, for I noticed many of the precepts that it contains are similar to some that Kano so enthusiastically championed in his own subsequent writings. In addition, Kano's oft mentioned *san iku shugi* or three educations: acquirement of knowledge, study of morality and physical education were possibly adapted from the teachings of Herbert Spencer.

Also, Spencer's theories on education stress that children should be taught to become individuals who contribute to the good of society. Moreover, Kano mentions that the spirit of the Kodokan membership was one based on self-reliance. For instance, he himself soldiered on for several difficult years before soliciting funds for the upkeep and expansion of the Kodokan. This situation was brought upon when membership increased greatly and magazine publication costs became too onerous for him to bear alone.

As we have repeatedly seen above, Kano the academic was ever eager to teach important lessons to his students. Since there were too few schools and fewer institutes of higher learning in his day this lack of adequate educational facilities seems to have concerned him deeply for quite naturally this was a major obstacle to Japan's social progress. Perhaps that is one of the reasons why Kano sought to educate his many Kodokan students academically in addition to instructing them in judo and in his efforts to establish a university in Kyushu. Some of Kano's early judo students seem to have been from underprivileged backgrounds and were thus in dire need of education, for Kano tells us that both Tsunejiro Tomita and Shiro Saigo, the first of his students to be awarded black belt grade, lived at the Kodokan, were later adopted, and as such were obliged to change their surnames. He also mentions that parents of some of his other students were unable to pay tuition fees for the education of their children at Kano Juku.

The content of Kano's lectures and his many essay publications were mostly centered on providing sound values and useful knowledge, especially so in helping his students to cope in daily life. In addition to the written word, he chose to impart this knowledge partly by means of judo, for he sought to instill in the young the virtues of courage, toughness and frugality that he believed would best help them to achieve in the wider world. Many of Kano's ex-students did in fact succeed to positions of responsibility, some in government service, in business and others particularly so in academia. By all accounts, therefore, he had a potent influence on the minds of his followers; for besides his leadership qualities, his students were no doubt inspired by the spirit of the man himself.

AFTERWORD
by
Brian N. Watson

We learned earlier that a number of ancient jujutsu warfare techniques were revised and molded by Kano in the 1880s into an offshoot of ju-jutsu, which eventually became the modern-day sporting activity of Kodokan judo. Interestingly enough, Kano mentions that before his creation of judo, the training sessions at most jujutsu schools were totally devoted to the study and practice of *kata* only. He states that over the centuries the sole objective of many practicing jujutsu men, especially those who possessed expensive weapons, changed radically from one focused on the techniques used for the mere summary, brutal coup de grace of one's foe, to that of the perfection of an art form in which the fluid and skilled performance of the prior de-fending and counter attacking swordsmanship expertise became paramount. This favored method of training in *kata,* as opposed to *randori*-type practice, doubtless had two notable advantages: it preserved many of the basic skills of jujutsu, while at the same time it eliminated almost completely the danger of accidental injury to the combatants. This change of emphasis may also have had the psychological effect of refining to some extent the characters of the practitioners, transforming them from mere out and out killers, into men of some virtue. Thus, many of these jujutsu schools gained in popularity and continued to thrive on account of the relatively safe environment and spiritually satisfying experience that they afforded their fee-paying students. Furthermore, because the shoguns of the Tokugawa era had maintained rela-tive peace throughout the nation from 1603 to 1867, there had been little need for the military class to include the more practical *randori*-type jujutsu training regimen in acute readiness for any actual armed conflict.

Following its introduction at the 1964 Tokyo Olympic Games, Kodokan judo has been a regularly staged Olympic event ever since the Munich games of 1972. This development resulted in global publicity for the sport, which is now reportedly practiced by over six million people in some 200 countries and regions, thus making it one of the most popular of the participant sports. What repercussions has this enormous expansion had on society worldwide? To give but one indication: although the population of Japan is more than twice that of France; today, more French people practice judo than do Japanese. Even so, to try to answer this question more fully, I think it best to focus on Japanese society because Japan's judo enthusiasts quite naturally have had greater access to and a resulting deeper understanding of Kano's teachings than have those of any other nation.

However, we must also keep in mind the fact that Kano's five-year-long training in jujutsu was embarked upon initially for only one reason; namely, to enable him to become strong physically. It was not until he had achieved this ambition and then reflected both on the influences that his training experiences had had on him psychologically and on the urgent social need of the day to modernize and improve the condition of Japanese society that he began to formulate ideas for the creation of a new theoretical and technical system of physical education that he named Kodokan judo. Perhaps he believed that in order to improve society, one must start by improving the character of individuals first. He mentions that as a result of his training, some positive changes had occurred not only to his physical condition but also to his personality. He stated, for instance, that his character had changed in that he had become calmer and much less irritable in his dealings with others.

When coaches analyze the progress of their sportsmen, they usually divide them into groups of three: the beginners, the intermediates and the advanced. Instructors typically consider ways of elevating the level of skill of their charges and often try to make them physically stronger. Rarely is serious consideration given to ways of cultivating the minds and developing the characters of these three groups of sporting aspirants. Kano's thinking on these groupings with regard to their progress in judo training, however, was different and rather profound, for he described these three levels of advancement in the following terms, and I quote, 'The three levels of judo are – training for defense against attack, cultivation of both mind and body, and putting one's energy to good use. We have also affirmed judo's highest goal as that of self-perfection for the betterment of society. For the sake of convenience, let us place the foundation – training for defense against attack – at the bottom and call it lower-level judo. Let us call training and cultivation, which are by-products of training for defense against attack, middle-level judo. The study of how to put one's energy to use in society comes last, so let us call it upper-level judo.

'When we divide judo into these three levels, we can see that it must not be limited to training for fighting in the dojo, and even if you train your body and cultivate your mind, if you do not go to the highest level, you cannot truly benefit society. No matter how great a person you are, how superior your intelligence, or how strong your body, if you die without achieving anything, as the proverb says: "Unused treasure is wasted treasure." It can be said that you perfected yourself, but it cannot be said that you contributed to the improvement of society. I urge all practitioners of judo to recognize that it consists of these three levels and to undergo their training without undue emphasis of one aspect over another. In lower-level judo the purpose of training is to learn how to defend against attack. At this level bare hands only are used for most of the training, but weapons are sometimes used for *kata*. However, recently I have come to believe that in judo training for small children, inflatable swords made of rubber or cloth rather than bamboo swords should be used right from the start to teach *kata* in which they learn to strike or thrust at each other and to fend off such blows. That is to say, I would like to incorporate some of the *kata* that were formerly taught in kendo into judo training in some form.

'By rights, spears, halberds, and other weapons used for the purpose of defending against attack should be included in judo. Swords and stout sticks, however, have the most uses as weapons, and kendo is one of the essential elements of judo, so should be included in judo in some form. It is necessary not only as *kata* but also in competition.

'In the future I believe judo will incorporate some of the *kata* from the current kendo into ordinary training, but I believe the current kendo, as it stands now, is less than satisfactory. Swords are no longer considered as useful as they once were. Compared to what is learned in judo, there are no situations in which having a sword is an advantage, except when you draw the sword and take up a defensive posture. Without knowledge of judo, even those who use swords will be unable to wield them with any great skill or confidence. On the contrary, practitioners of kendo will gradually recognize the need to learn judo at the same time. Thus, I believe the current judo and kendo should be integrated.

'Of course, there may also be considerable opposition to this idea, so it may be difficult to do this right away. However, the general trend is certainly heading in that direction. But as time passes there will inevitably be a distinction made between those who attach importance to swords and those who play down their importance.

'In the future, those who practice the fighting arts such as boxing will have to put in as much effort as judo practitioners. I believe it would also be of value to practitioners of sumo and savate to do some study of judo. But the method naturally differs depending on whether these are practiced merely for the purpose of fighting or for physical education. When these are practiced for physical education, they are already at the middle level. As for what can be done at the middle level, apart from physical education, opportunities for various types of training should be used and the mind should be cultivated. This entails watching how other people train, and, by observing various skills and devising ways to put them to use, training your mind and body, controlling your emotions, and developing courage. In short, this means becoming able to control your body and mind at will.

'In order to carry out this training of the body and cultivation of the mind, there are other things that can be called by-products of practice. These include the contented feeling that is gained following practice, the struggle of competition, and the pleasure that comes from mastering a skill. If you advance even further, you have an opportunity to observe skillful *kata* and to acquire aesthetic sentiments. I believe these should also be part of middle-level judo.

'Reaching upper-level judo means making the most effective use of the mental and physical energy you acquired at the lower and middle levels and contributing to the advancement of society. Thus, upper-level judo has the widest application and requires the most creativity. In daily activities also, whether or not something meets the aims of judo can easily be determined in each situation by considering whether or not you made the most effective use of your mental and physical energy. Everything human beings do can be evaluated based on these rules.

'Being physically weak is not necessarily an innate condition. In many cases, this is the result of doing something not in accord with these rules at a particular time. You must remember that failing to have a strong sense of timing and thus being unable to accept people is the result of neglecting to carry out the right mental training at the right time in the past. In many cases both people's successes and failures are determined by whether or not they made the necessary effort at the right time.

'As long as they believe that they have used their mental and physical energy most effectively, human beings will never lose hope, nor will they suffer undue anxiety. This is because, having used their energy most effectively, they have no room to expend it in any other manner. Feelings of regret and worry occur when you have not done what you should have, or when you cannot make up your mind to do what you should. In the future I would like to apply the principles of judo to all forms of human behavior and conduct research on this topic. I would also urge people to practice judo to help overcome the mental fatigue that results from regret and anxiety.'

When Kano opened the Kodokan, he was certainly fired by lofty ideals. He states that he taught his students free of charge and that he spent his own money on the upkeep of the Kodokan. For a young graduate, these were certainly challenges for him to attempt alone, or did he receive assistance from others? Although I have found no evidence to the contrary, because he was only twenty-one at the time, I cannot help wondering that he may have had some moral and financial support in these early endeavors.

We have seen that in the earliest days judo developed hesitantly on account of Kano's repeated relocations of the Kodokan to larger and more convenient premises. In the mid 1890s judo's popularity was quickly spreading and by the 1900s Kano mentions, somewhat surprisingly, that 6,000 or so young Japanese men were already regularly engaged in training. Over the next two to three decades, primarily in response to the founding of the Judokai in 1922, later to be re-named the Kodokan Culture Council; and as a result of the further organizational development of the Kodokan administration, hundreds of branch dojos were opened in the nation's state-run schools, police stations, military camps, universities, and in private corporations, as well as a small number set up in foreign countries. This successful early promotion was, of course, chiefly due to the earnest efforts that Kano put into not only teaching his art but also, and perhaps more importantly, into his many writings on judo and other relevant topics that he contributed to specialist magazines. Nonetheless, I doubt that Kano himself could have achieved such speedy growth in the diffusion of judo in such a short time span without the strong support he increasingly received from his growing band of influential and wealthy associates. His backers at this time included such prominent men as the leading Japanese power broker of the day, Eiichi Shibusawa, who was a former Finance Minister, wealthy industrialist, philanthropist and later auditor and trustee of the Kodokan, together with Viscount Yajiro Shinagawa, Kaishu Katsu, and a number of other notables. In addition, Kano was able to garner co-operation from his many connections in sporting circles, as a founder and the first chairman of the Japan Amateur Sports Association, and as Japan's, and indeed, Asia's first member of the International Olympic Committee. Furthermore, I believe that there was another significant reason for Kano's success. As mentioned above, from the latter part of the 19th century, Japan had embarked on a somewhat frenzied nationwide quest of modernization. This was mostly a blanket attempt to overtake the leading Western nations of the day. One of the prime requisites for attaining such a large-scale undertaking was the formation of a healthy, strong and more especially a better-educated populace, chiefly so in the sciences. Therefore, this government-backed policy synergized well with Kano's fervent desire to reform parts of the Japanese education system, in particular, compulsory education, and to promote the wider practice of Olympic sports as well as judo, which eventually contributed in some measure to improvement in the general health of the nation. In this endeavor, he received both moral and sporadic financial support not only from key sporting and business leaders but later from prominent political figures also.

Incidentally, while translating the above-mentioned references to Kano's rules to be observed by students of Kano Juku, I was reminded of the well-known Japanese proverb '*Bunbu Ryodo*', a phrase that means 'Culture and Martial Power, Both Ways Together'. This concept is a very old ideal and one held in esteem in Japan, both culture and power united together; for the rationale is that culture without power will be ineffectual whereas power without culture will be barbarous. It seems that Kano believed very much in the message contained in this well-known saying. He himself exemplified this ideal by his training in jujutsu, creating judo and by devoting most of his life to the furtherance of education. In fact I noticed that he used the essence of this proverb as his motto for Kano Juku also: 'The path to true greatness lies in the pursuit of the military and the literary arts.' The strict rules and Spartan life-style that his Kano Juku students were made to abide by may seem a little harsh to modern-day readers, particularly those in the West. Nevertheless his methods did yield fruit, for many of Kano's students later distinguished themselves by attaining responsible leadership roles in Japanese society.

Kano tells us that the contributors to the Kodokan magazines were professors, diplomats, lawyers, engineers, and other professionals as well as sportsmen. These monthlies, which were edited by Kano, contained some 160 pages, which attest to the hard work that must have regularly gone into the tasks of both editing and publishing these periodicals. Judging by the wide range of specialist topics that these magazines contained, it would seem that in addition to Kano Juku, Kano was in fact extending the curriculum of his juku to include Kodokan training, thus creating an academy or a quasi judo college as such. He says that after a few years though, he ran into financial difficulties and had to use increasing amounts of his own assets not only for the maintenance of the Kodokan but also in an effort to keep the loss-making magazines afloat. This gives a clear indication as to the seriousness and to the extent of his commitment. Ultimately, however, adverse circumstances forced him to change some of the content and the titles of these magazines and to cease publication of others.

When viewing photographs of early Kodokan judo training sessions, I noticed that by far the vast majority of Kano's trainees were teenage boys. The above-mentioned articles in *Sako* and *Yuko no Katsudo* magazines, a number of which I have browsed through at the Kodokan library, were written on a literary level that was more attuned to mature adults than to youths. This leads me to think that some of these essays were no doubt difficult to comprehend for Kano's young judo aspirants, since many of them would not have had knowledge of a sufficient number of ideograms with which to appreciate fully the content. Therefore, perhaps this was one of the reasons why circulations dwindled over time and Kano in due course faced growing financial problems.

Yet despite this unfortunate turn of events, Kano continued to have increasing success in attracting newcomers to take up the art of Kodokan judo. His subsequent plans to introduce and then expand the popularity of judo abroad, however, initially met with a much less favorable response. The biggest obstacles seem to have been both linguistic and financial. For instance, the Japanese custom of each branch dojo paying a head tax to the main dojo, in this case the Kodokan, was not so well received among overseas judo club members, and the formidable language barrier, particularly so in the non-English speaking nations, presented setbacks. Lecturing and demonstrating judo techniques in English on the physical plane was for Kano, being competent in English, a relatively simple matter. Explaining his theories of judo on the intellectual and moral planes in written form, especially in other languages, however, was more of a challenge, not only for Kano but also for his like-minded judo pioneers. Nonetheless, progress was made, chiefly so from 1900 to the 1920s when the diffusion of judo in the U.S. and in Europe was being increasingly instigated. By the 1930s, a growing interest in judo continued to spread to several more countries, particularly so in the West. However, the outbreak of hostilities involving Japanese and Chinese troops in Manchuria in the 1930s, the cancellation of the scheduled 1940 Tokyo Summer Olympic Games and the start of the Pacific War in 1941 all culminated in a sharp decrease of international support for and interest in Japan and her culture. This was a period when Japan went almost completely into the dark and where she so remained till the late 1950s.

It was not until the announcement was made that judo would be introduced at the 1964 Tokyo Summer Olympic Games, long after Kano's demise in 1938, that his dream of judo attaining universal recognition finally began to be realized. Thereafter, the numbers of enthusiasts in foreign countries forming national judo associations mushroomed rapidly, a trend that still continues today, albeit at a much slower pace. Apart from the endeavors of Kano and his leading students, some dedicated foreigners also made efforts to promote judo, particularly from the mid 1940s onwards. So much so that by the early 1950s both the European Judo Union and the International Judo Federation had been established and were gradually starting to assume the Kodokan's erstwhile role of leading the worldwide expansion of the sport.

A question that I sought to answer here in relation to individuals was this: Did the judo training experiences of the three below-mentioned experts help them in anyway to achieve their varied accomplishments in life? Naturally, this is a difficult question to answer. There are so many variables. All one can hope to do, as I have tried to do here, is to give facts relevant to their experiences and to list some of their successes. I define success here, incidentally, to mean both achievement and contentment in life in the broadest sense, not necessarily in the accumulation of great wealth. A man launching a business may in due course gain from the enterprise a reasonable standard of living, another may pursue a career and eventually become renowned in his particular vocation, likewise a mother may succeed in raising a family of healthy and able children, for example.

Among the many who were profoundly influenced by Kano's teachings and who achieved success both in life and in judo were a number of men whom

I knew personally, the three I wish to comment on in particular are representative: an Englishman, an American and a Japanese man. The Englishman, Trevor Pryce Leggett (1914-2000), a Kodokan 6th dan, became a noted oriental scholar, Japanese-language translator and author of over thirty full-length books, some incidentally, written in Japanese. Following an initial interest in judo, Leggett came to have great interest in and admiration for other facets of Eastern culture; his many writings included works on Buddhism, yoga, Zen and *shogi* (Japanese chess). He was, in his younger days, a single handicap golfer, chess player and later gained from the Japan Shogi Federation a 5th dan at *shogi*. Born in London, he graduated from the University of London (LL. B.) in 1934. His father was leading violinist for the famed British conductor of the day Sir Thomas Beecham. In early life Leggett trained with a view to becoming a concert pianist and as such did little, if any, physical exercise. Being on occasions sickly, his doctor advised him to take up some sport. At the age of 16, therefore, the sport he chose was judo and he started taking lessons at the London Budokwai. After training under the famous judo masters Yukio Tani and Gunji Koizumi, he made swift progress and had reached 3rd dan grade prior to his gaining a post at the British embassy in Tokyo in 1939. While in Japan he trained at both the Chuo University judo club and the Kodokan. With the flare-up of the Pacific War in 1941, Leggett, along with other diplomats and foreign nationals, was interned before being repatriated in 1942. He then saw military service in India, where he was required to interrogate Japanese prisoners of war. Following this episode, he joined the British Broadcasting Corporation in London and from 1946 to 1970 served as head of the BBC's Japanese Service where he was responsible for the content of Japanese language short-wave radio broadcasts beamed from the UK to Japan.

Leggett was a man of strong character, which no doubt contributed to his achievements throughout life. Were these efforts influenced by or linked in anyway to his long years of training in judo? He himself seemed to think so, for like Kano; Leggett was totally dedicated to the furtherance of judo and to education, and as such encouraged many youths, mainly British, to engage in the sport. In the U.K. he often wrote, broadcast and lectured on Japanese culture and also in the Japanese language when being interviewed by media personnel during his occasional visits to Japan.

His influence among the judo fraternity in Britain was quite extensive, from administrative responsibilities that included membership of the British Judo Association's Technical Board, to the day to day instruction at the grass roots level. I recall, for instance, that for the British national judo team members and those of black belt grade who were allowed to attend his popular weekly Sunday Class at the Budokwai in the 1950s and 1960s, he made but one rule: all had to arrive at the dojo wearing a suit, white shirt with a stiffly-starched detachable white collar and especially a necktie. Also, at the end of judo classes at his London dojo, the Renshuden, he would always give us a pep talk, sometimes on judo but more often advice on other things in life. After his strenuous judo training sessions, he would regularly accompany his trainees to a local coffee shop or restaurant, never to a bar, and teach them how to play chess. He encouraged the young black belt holders, especially those who planned to train in Japan, to write essays for him and would edit their efforts following the meal; he also gave us advice on Japanese language study and taught us the rudiments of the written language. He once remarked that the challenge in life that he had found the hardest to master was that of judo. In 1984, Leggett was awarded the Order of the Sacred Treasure by the government of Japan for his contributions in helping to introduce Japanese culture to Britain.

Trevor Pryce Leggett
(1914-2000)
Judoman-scholar

Another man who was very much influenced by Kano and who was totally dedicated to training in martial arts during the 1950s and 1960s was the illustrious budoman, Donn F. Draeger (1922-1982), a native of Milwaukee, Wisconsin, U.S.A. He gave much initial help and guidance to young foreign judo men who had made their way to Japan, particularly those who had arrived with little money but with big determination. Draeger, fascinated by the martial spirit of budo, first trained in judo and became one of the earliest non-Japanese to gain a coveted Kodokan 5th dan grade. He later earned a 7th dan in kendo, a 7th dan in iai-do, (art of sword-drawing) and a 7th dan in jodo (stick fighting). A major in the U.S. Marine Corps before retirement, he became technical director of the magazine Martial Arts International. In the 1960s and the 1970s Draeger traveled much in Asia. He subsequently became a noted historian of classical Asian martial disciplines and penned over twenty well-researched books, some of which are now regarded as authoritative works on a wide variety of antagonistic arts. He was, incidentally, martial arts coordinator and stunt double for British actor Sean Connery in the 1967 James Bond motion picture You Only Live Twice. In his later years, Draeger did substantial research on, and propagated interest in, the early development of traditional weaponry. Succumbing to cancer at the Tripler Army Medical Center in Honolulu, Hawaii on October 20, 1982, he was later buried at Wood National Cemetery, Milwaukee.

Donn F. Draeger
(1922-1982)
Judoman-scholar

A Japanese man, who after early difficulties achieved particular success both in life and in judo, was Nobuo Murakami (1921-2005) a Kodokan 6th dan, one of the founders of the Marunouchi Judo Club, Tokyo, and for many years Japan's leading chef of French cuisine. He was also, for some twenty-seven years, Head Chef and Executive Advisor to the board of directors of the

Imperial Hotel, Tokyo.

Murakami started taking lessons in judo at the age of ten. The following year both of his parents died of illness within months of each other. He therefore had to leave primary school and was sent by his uncle to work at a nearby coffee shop, where he washed dishes. After similar employment at a succession of restaurants, he joined the Imperial Hotel in 1939 and rose to become a cook. In 1942 he was conscripted into the Japanese Army and sent to China and Korea where he saw action. Upon suffering leg wounds, he was captured by Russian troops and detained in a prisoner of war camp in Siberia. Unlike hundreds of his compatriots, he survived the harsh conditions and following repatriation in 1947, he returned once more to the kitchens of the Imperial Hotel. He married one year later. In 1952 he gained a judo first dan and in 1954 a second dan.

In 1955, the management of the Imperial Hotel appointed Murakami to work as a cook at the Japanese Embassy in Belgium and in the ensuing year he was sent to the Ritz Hotel, Paris, to learn the art of French cuisine. Having little prior facility with the French language, he made great use of a French-Japanese dictionary in an attempt to further his understanding. Later, however, much speedier progress was made after he was called upon to act as judo coach to the hotel's French chefs, and they, out of appreciation, taught him the many secrets of their culinary expertise.

Following further training in both Milan, Italy, and Stockholm, Sweden, he returned home in 1958, and soon thereafter his career spectacularly took off. Being the pioneer French chef of his day, he devoted himself to disseminating his knowledge of western cuisine to the Japanese public and chiefly owing to the long and successful run of his TV series, *Kyo no Ryori*, (Today's Dishes), which was broadcast nationwide by NHK, Murakami soon became a household name. Later on, he received a further key accolade when appointed head of catering at the Olympic Village, where he was responsible for the daily preparation of some 20,000 meals for all competitors and officials attending the 1964 Tokyo Summer Olympic Games. Murakami later encouraged his culinary subordinates at the Imperial Hotel to take up judo training. This was an attempt to make them mentally and physically stronger, which no doubt helped them somewhat when having to lift and carry the many heavy pots and pans around the hot and busy kitchens of the hotel. In subsequent years Murakami was the subject of numerous press interviews. He also published his own writings on events in his life as well as several books on the technical aspects of French cuisine. In recognition of his efforts in helping to promote Franco-Japanese intercultural exchange, Murakami gained a number of prestigious awards from French culinary associations and in 1994 the Order of the Sacred Treasure, 4th class, was conferred on him by the Japanese government.

Other judo enthusiasts who achieved notable fame in their chosen vocational fields include Takashi Ishihara, 2nd dan, a former President of Nissan Motors and a former Chairman of the Japan Automobile Manufacturers Association, and Hiroshi Okuda, 4th dan, ex-chairman of the motor manufacturer, Toyota, and ex-chairman of the influential Keidanren, the Japan Employers' Association. A number of judo devotees who are internationally well known in political circles include William Hague, one-time leader of the British Conservative Party, the late Pierre Trudeau and Brian Mulroney, both erstwhile prime ministers of Canada and Vladimir Putin, 6th dan, President of Russia. Putin is, incidentally, honorary president of the EJU (European Judo Union) and in 2004 co-authored a judo manual publication, *Judo: History, Theory, Practice.* Currently one of the world's most famous politicians, Angela Merkel, Germany's first female Chancellor, also trained in judo and holds a black belt.

Finally, the monumental social changes that have occurred in Japan since the founding of the Kodokan in 1882, have quite naturally greatly transformed the activities of this institution, too. Apart from it still being regarded as the most esteemed judo grading authority, its significance as a judo training center, however, started to diminish somewhat at the end of World War II when in 1945 the US-led occupation forces ordered the closure of budo training halls nationwide. Some three years later, in 1948, General Headquarter authorities relaxed this blanket ban. Martial arts practice halls were re-opened and competitive events were resumed. At that time, a small number of university judo clubs quickly became recognized as Japan's principal judo training centers of excellence, whereas the Kodokan's activities became increasingly focused on judo-related administrative duties.

Kodokan International Judo Center
Kasuga, Bunkyo-ku, Tokyo

Those who normally practice judo at the Kodokan these days are for the most part office workers, both male and female, and children who attend evening sessions between the hours of 5 p.m. to 7:30 p.m. Monday to Saturday. The facilities available to members include the use of several dojos, both large and some small teaching dojos, a restaurant, a library of some 7,000 works, a reading room, a moderately-sized museum, a dormitory for the out of town trainees, and a book shop. Apart from the traditional Kodokan events held, such as the Kagami Biraki ceremony, the mid-winter *kangeiko* and mid-summer *shochugeiko* training sessions, the monthly grading contests, the Red & White Team Competition and the occasional staging of a championship event, the Kodokan today maintains a fairly modest day to day role. This institution, which started life as a *machi* dojo in 1882, seems to have completed a full circle. Currently many of the practice sessions held there are for beginners and intermediates and are often evocative of the low-key atmosphere prevailing at a typical *machi* dojo rather than the Mecca of judo in terms of a training center, for rarely do the Japan national team members use any of the Kodokan's facilities for training purposes these days.

Before I took up training in judo in England many years ago, I recall asking a senior member of my local judo club, 'What is judo?' His glib reply was, 'Wrestling with jackets.' In those days, most of my contemporaries believed this and practiced judo in exactly such a manner, many still do, for apart from the few judo manuals then available, we were not aware of any books expounding Kano's theories. It is my hope, therefore, that in future more of Kano's writings will be translated from Japanese into foreign languages; so that the international sporting fraternity will come to understand clearly his ideas and aspirations with regard to sport, to education and to the underlying purpose of his efforts: helping one to achieve self-fulfillment.

GLOSSARY

Atemiwaza

Blows directed at anatomically vulnerable parts of an assailant's body by means of some weapon or by the use of open hand, fist, finger, elbow, knee and foot.

Bakufu

The shogunate government. Headed by a line of shogun military dictators from 1192 until the establishment of the Meiji government in 1868.

Beecham, Sir Thomas (1879-1961)

Musician and orchestral conductor. Born at St. Helens, Lancashire, the elder son of Sir Joseph Beecham. Founded the London Philharmonic Orchestra in 1932. Appointed artistic director of Covent Garden from 1932 to 1939.

Bojutsu

An ancient art of fighting with staves of varying lengths. Although Bojutsu is not as popular as other martial arts in modern-day Japan, it is still commonly practiced by police officers who sometimes resort to the use of staves when apprehending criminals, especially those armed with weapons such as knives or swords.

Budo

The switch from the classical battlefield *bujutsu* or *bugei* (arts of self-protection) into the *budo* (arts of self-perfection) began to flourish prior to and continued during the modernization of Japan in the Meiji era (1868-1912). The objectives and character of the *budo* arts were essentially different from the pure violence associated with *jutsu* and stressed the philosophical tenets of the *do* or 'way of life'. Judo was derived from *jujutsu*, kendo from *kenjutsu*, aikido from *aikijutsu*, and so forth.

Bugei

All of the classical military arts used in ancient warfare are usually classed as either *bugei* or *bujutsu*. These include *jujutsu*, *kenjutsu*, *bajutsu* or horseman-ship, *kyujutsu* or bowmanship, *sojutsu* or spear fighting and others.

Bujutsu

Classical military arts. See *Bugei*.

Butokukai

In 1895, the Butokukai (officially named *Dai Nippon Butokukai)* was estab-lished in Kyoto. Later, branch dojos were set up in prefectures nationwide. In 1905, the *Budo Senmon Gakko* was founded within the framework of the *Dai Nippon Butokukai* for the purpose of training judo and kendo teachers. In 1911, the *Bujutsu Senmon Gakko* was created within the *Dai Nippon Butokukai* to administer all martial arts training throughout Japan. Shortly thereafter, the Ministry of Education made judo and kendo training compulsory subjects for junior high school boys. Militarists allegedly infiltrated the Butokukai in 1941 during the hostilities of World War II when all budo in Japan was subordi-nated to the war effort. Firearms and bayonet training were then introduced. From 1945 to 1950 training in such military-style disciplines was banned nationwide by order of the Supreme Commander of Allied Powers.

Confucianism

A tradition of Chinese origin said to have been known in Japan since the 5th century. Although it has religious connotations, it is mainly a philosophi-cal, ethical, and political teaching. In Japan it assumed particular importance during the 6th to 9th centuries and again from the Edo period (1600-1867) through to the Showa period (1926-1989).

Count Katsu

Adopted son of Kaishu Katsu.

Dan

Any of twelve degrees of advancing proficiency in judo, although only ten have ever been awarded. This system of grading judo practitioners was devised by Jigoro Kano in 1883 and was adopted by adherents of other martial disciplines and later by followers of Japanese cultural pursuits such as calligraphy, *shogi*, *igo*, etc.

Densho

These are both oral and written instructions containing secret information on the techniques of a traditional Japanese art, especially the skills devised for teaching at jujutsu schools. Customarily the *densho* are passed on from master to a student on his gaining proficiency in the art.

Dojo

Often translated into English as sports training hall or gymnasium, it has, however, other connotations. The word 'dojo' comes from the Buddhist tradition and is a room for the training of the mind as well as the body. In other words, it is a place where one receives instruction from one's teacher in an art or in some religious discipline.

Eastlake, F. Washington (1858-1905)

American professor of English who trained in judo. Arrived in Japan in 1884, publisher of an English language newspaper and founder of an English language school in Kanda, Tokyo, in 1888.

Edo

The former name of Tokyo. Edo was changed to that of Tokyo in 1868 coinciding with the establishment of the Meiji government.

Eishoji

Small Jodo Buddhist temple, located in Shitaya Kita Inari-cho, (present-day Higashi Ueno, Daito-ku,) Tokyo. Jigoro Kano established the Kodokan at Eishoji in May 1882.

Emperor Meiji and the Imperial Rescript on Education

Emperor Meiji, who fulfilled the Meiji Restoration in 1868, thus terminating a long period of military rule and replacing a feudal system that had lasted for some 680 years, was keen to establish a national education system and to promote morality in order to modernize Japan. The "Imperial Rescript on Education" was issued to illustrate the moral principles that each citizen should follow. A copy of this document was sent, together with a photograph of Emperor Meiji, for display in all schools throughout the Japanese Empire. This rescript served as a very powerful tool of political indoctrination and remained in effect until the end of World War II.

English Translation of the Imperial Rescript on Education

Our Imperial Ancestors have founded our Empire on a basis broad and everlasting and have deeply and firmly implanted virtue; our subjects ever united in loyalty and filial piety have from generation to generation illustrated the beauty thereof. This is the glory of the fundamental character of our Empire, and herein also lays the source of our education. Be filial to your parents, affectionate to your brothers and sisters; as husbands and wives be harmonious, as friends true; bear yourselves in modesty and moderation; extend your benevolence to all; pursue learning and cultivate arts, and thereby develop intellectual faculties and perfect moral powers; furthermore, advance public good and promote common interests; always respect the Constitution and observe the laws; should emergency arise, offer yourselves courageously to the State; and thus guard and maintain the prosperity of our Imperial Throne coeval with heaven and earth. So shall you not only be our good and faithful subjects but render illustrious the best traditions of your forefathers. The Way here set forth is indeed the teaching bequeathed by our Imperial Ancestors, to be observed alike by Their Descendants and the subjects, infallible for all ages and true in all places. It is our wish to lay it to heart in all reverence, in common with you, our subjects, that we may thus attain to the same virtue.

30 October 1890
(Imperial Signature, Imperial Seal)

Enomoto, Takeaki (1836-1908)

Military man and politician. In 1856, he studied at the Nagasaki Naval Training Center, and later became an instructor at the Tsukiji Warship Training Center. In 1862, he went to Rotterdam, Holland, to further his studies and to supervise construction of the *Kaiyo Maru* warship, which had been commissioned by the Shogunate. While there, he realized that the telegraph would become an important means of communication and after returning to Japan, planned a system to connect Edo (Tokyo) to Yokohama using two Morse telegraph machines made by the French Jinnei Company.

Fukuda, Hachinosuke (1827-1879)

Kano's first regular jujutsu teacher. He taught Kano the Tenjin Shinyo style which includes many effective groundwork techniques some of which Kano incorporated into Kodokan judo.

Gakushuin

A school established in 1877 for the education of members of the imperial family and the nobility. In 1947, following the abolition of the peerage system, it became a private educational institution, open to the public. Renamed Gakushuin University, it is located in Toshima Ward, Tokyo, and today has a student enrollment of over 7,000.

Genoa Conference

Representatives of 30 European nations convened in Genoa, Italy, on April 10, 1922 to attempt the reconstruction of European finance and commerce. It was the first such conference after World War I in which Germany and the Soviet Union were accepted on a par with other nations.

Go no Kata

The *kata* of hardness & strength contained ten techniques. It was developed in 1887 and was taught for a time at the Kodokan. The techniques are performed in *jigotai* (defensive posture) and include throws, strangles, wrist and arm locks and *atemiwaza*. This *kata* is intended to demonstrate the correct use of strength in contrast to the principle of 'softness or yielding' as demonstrated in *Ju no Kata*. Jigoro Kano, however, became dissatisfied with *Go no Kata* and was of the opinion that it be revised. It is rarely taught or performed today.

Hakama
Japanese style garment worn by both sexes, covering the legs from waist to ankles. Men wear wide-pleated trousers and females pleated skirts.

Hamilton, Sir William (1788-1856)
British philosopher, born in Ireland, influential figure in Scottish philosophical circles, published works on logic, philosophy, literature and physics, professor of history at Edinburgh University 1821-1856.

Hirose, Takeo (1868-1904)
Studied judo under Kano, naval commander, hero in the 1904-1905 Russo-Japanese War.

Honda, Masujiro (1866-1925)
A student of Kano Juku, where he assisted Kano in the teaching of judo. Honda became one of Japan's leading authorities on English language and literature. He promoted education, charitable causes, the study of English, and was active as a writer, journalist and translator. He translated *Black Beauty* by Anna Sewell (1820-1877) into Japanese. Engaged as a professor at Tokyo University of Foreign Languages, he also served as a diplomat (member of the Japanese delegation to the Paris Peace Conference in 1920) and interpreter (interpreted for H.R.H. Edward, Prince of Wales, during his official visit to Japan in 1922).

Iikubo, Tsunetoshi (1835-1889)
Kano's third regular jujutsu master. He taught Kano the Kito style, which includes some effective throwing techniques that Kano later incorporated into Kodokan judo.

Imagawakoji
Former name of a district in present-day Kanda, Tokyo.

Inagaki, Manjiro (1861-1908)
Former student of Kano. Diplomat and writer. Studied in England at Cambridge University 1888-1890. First Deputy Minister in Siam (Thailand).

Inoue, Kowashi (1843-1895)

Educator and politician, he became Minister of Education in March 1893. Inoue introduced a number of radical reforms to Japan's education system that improved in particular vocational training for youths. He was instrumental in the founding of technical schools specializing in agriculture, sericulture, forestry, veterinary science and fisheries.

Iso, Masatomo (1819-1881)

The Tenjin Shinyo jujutsu master who taught Kano following the death of Hachinosuke Fukuda, Kano's first regular jujutsu master.

Jita Kyoei

Jita Kyoei, mutual benefit for oneself and others, is one of the two ideals (the other being *seiryoku zenyo*) that Kano identified as the two highest goals that judoka should abide by in order to contribute to the betterment of society.

Judoka

One who practices the art of judo.

Jujutsu

An ancient, Japanese martial art in which a wide variety of secret armed and unarmed throwing, striking, and restraining techniques are employed in order to subdue, paralyze, maim or kill one's foe.

Juku

A private, preparatory school, that usually offers instruction to students in academic subjects, art or sports.

Ju yoku go o seisu

A well-known principle of judo, exemplified in Ju no Kata, suggests that the soft or flexible can overcome the hard and powerful. Thus, by using the principles of flexibility and the opponent's own force, a man of small stature is able to overcome a bigger man.

Kagami Biraki

A traditional celebration formerly observed by samurai families and held annually on the second Sunday of January at the Kodokan to mark the opening of the dojo for the New Year.

Kamei, Eizaburo (1864-1913)

Former student of Kano. Statesman. Born in Kumamoto, Kyushu, the son of a samurai of the Kumamoto Clan. In 1888, he graduated from the Law College of Tokyo Imperial University and successively held offices as counselor of the Cabinet Legislation Bureau and prefectural governor of Tokushima, Shizuoka and Miyagi prefectures. In 1908, when the second Katsura Cabinet was in power, he became Superintendent-General of the Metropolitan Police Department. In 1911 he was selected by Imperial nomination as a member of the House of Peers.

Kamidana

Literally 'god shelf'. A wooden shelf, which serves as a household altar on which a miniature shrine, fruit, vegetation or other offerings are placed. Most budo dojos, factories, offices and homes display a Kamidana. In times of need, Japanese customarily offer prayers to the Kamidana in order to seek divine protection.

Kangeiko

A month-long series of hard training sessions held in the early morning and evening in mid-winter, especially by practitioners of judo and kendo. Kangeiko has been held annually at the Kodokan since 1894. Rather than attempting to improve one's technique, the main objective is to strengthen one's willpower. Devotees of other traditional Japanese arts such as flower arrangement, tea ceremony, etc., also observe Kangeiko.

Kano Juku

This was Kano's preparatory school that he established in February 1882 on the premises of Eishoji, where he taught academic subjects and later judo. In existence until 1920, the motto of Kano Juku was: *The path to true greatness lies in the study of both the military and the literary arts.* Some 350 students attended over the years, including the writer and translator Masujiro Honda

(1866-1925). Its purpose was strongly oriented towards cultivating not only skill in judo but also the virtues of courage, toughness and frugality.

Kappo

Traditional Japanese methods of resuscitation used in an attempt to revive a person who has lost consciousness.

Kata

A slow-motion performance by both attacker and defender of pre-arranged armed or unarmed martial arts techniques.

Katsu, Kaishu (1823-1899)

Also known as Yasuyoshi Katsu, trained in swordsmanship from boyhood, he was active in the transition from the Tokugawa shogunate to the Meiji government. A leading scholar, statesman, naval commander and in 1860, aboard the vessel *Kanrin Maru,* he headed the first Japanese mission to the U.S.A.

Kenjutsu

An ancient art of sword fighting. The swordsman was trained in the use of three weapons: the odachi (long curved sword), the kodachi (short straight sword) and the tanto (dagger). Whereas modern kendo is widely regarded as the sporting offshoot of Japanese swordsmanship, kenjutsu included the violent jujutsu techniques of the battlefield.

Kime no kata

Imitation weapons are used in this combative kata. It was devised to teach methods of defending oneself against an armed or unarmed assailant. Eight of the techniques are performed while the performers are in the formal Japanese-style sitting position and twelve are performed while they are standing.

Kobusho

A martial arts training center for samurai, founded by the shogun in 1856 in Tsukiji, Tokyo. Later, Kobusho branches were established in Kanda and in other areas of Tokyo. Instruction was given in archery, spear fighting, fencing, jujutsu, gunnery, etc. In 1857, a Warship Operations Center was added. At its height, some 500 samurai were receiving instruction. In 1866, the Kobusho and Rikugunsho (Army Training Center) were amalgamated.

Kodokan Culture Council

Originally named 'Judokai', and established within the Kodokan in 1922, this Culture Council was formed for the promotion and development of Kodokan judo from spiritual, moral, and cultural perspectives. Although not currently active, it had departments responsible for general affairs, accounting, editing, seminars, research studies, the publication of books and advanced instructor training.

Kodokan Judo Institute

Headquarters of Kodokan judo founded in 1882 by Jigoro Kano at Eisho Temple, Tokyo. The name Ko-do-kan means 'the institute where one learns a way to live one's life'. Later, the Kodokan was moved to the following Tokyo locations: Minami Jimbocho, Kanda; Kami Ni Bancho, Kojimachi; Fujimicho, again to Kojimachi; Shimotomisaka-cho, Koishikawa; Sakashita-machi, in 1934 to Korakuen Ichichome, near Suidobashi Station; and in 1958 to its present site, Kasuga, Bunkyo-ku, Tokyo. To mark the 100th anniversary of its foundation, parts of the building were demolished, re-built and in 1984 the Kodokan was re-named Kodokan International Judo Center.

Kohaku Shiai (Red Team vs. White Team Competition)

Elimination contests for dan grades held annually in spring and autumn at the Kodokan. Competitors who perform exceptionally well in these contests and defeat ten or more opponents of equal grade in succession are upgraded automatically on the day, thus the customary ruling of a minimum 18-month period in grade of a 2nd dan before promotion to 3rd dan and the two-year period in grade of a 3rd dan before promotion to 4th dan are waived.

Koizumi, Gunji (1885-1965)

Master of Tenjin Shinyo jujutsu. An expert in Chinese lacquer ware, he ran a shop in central London. In 1918 he founded the London Budokwai where he and Yukio Tani taught judo, kendo and other Japanese arts to the British public. He published the book, *My Study of Judo*.

Koyata, Torio

A Meiji era political figure of the Choshu domain faction. He formed the Moderate Conservative Party (Hoshuto-Chuseiha).

Kuhara, Fusanosuke (1869-1965)

Business leader, politician, academic. Founder of Kuhara Mining Co., forerunner of the giant Hitachi conglomerate.

Kuzushi

Methods of disturbing the opponent's balance preceding the application of a throwing or ground work technique. Kano's research, development and emphasis on the principles of Kuzushi largely distinguish judo from jujutsu technique. Although Kano distanced judo from the violence associated with jujutsu, he did nevertheless preserve jujutsu skills. These can be seen in the judo katas. But unlike jujutsu, only imitation swords and daggers are employed in judo. Edged weapons are strictly prohibited.

Masutemi waza

The classification of throws in which the thrower deliberately sacrifices himself by falling to the mat on his back in the process of throwing his opponent.

Mill, John Stuart (1806-1873)

Philosopher and political economist. He was born in London and educated at home by his father, the philosopher, James Mill.

Miura, Goro (1847-1926)

One time Principal of Gakushuin. Army lieutenant general, Minister to Seoul, Korea, in 1895, allegedly hatched the plot, which resulted in a group of men invading the Kyongbok Palace to carry out the brutal killing of Queen Min and two other women on October 8, 1895. Miura was subsequently recalled to Japan, tried and acquitted on the grounds of insufficient evidence. He later became an influential politician, especially active during the Taisho era (1912-1926).

Mochi

Cakes of pounded rice. Often served on festive occasions, particularly at celebrations held to mark the start of the New Year.

Nango, Jiro
Nephew of Jigoro Kano. Since Kano's eldest son, Rishin, an artist, died at the age of 37, Nango was chosen as Jigoro Kano's immediate successor and headed the Kodokan from December 1938 to November 1946. The 3rd President was Risei Kano who served until February 1980 when Kano's grandson Yukimitsu Kano assumed the presidency.

Newaza
Judo grappling techniques applied when both fighters are either kneeling or lying on the mat.

Nogi, Maresuke (1849-1912)
In 1907, Nogi, an army general, became Principal of the Peers School (now Gakushuin University). The ritual suicide (seppuku) of Nogi and his wife, on 13 September 1912, following the death of Emperor Meiji, caused a sensation and was viewed by the public as a symbol of loyalty and sacrifice. Nogi's suicide had a profound impact on Japanese intellectuals, in particular the famous writers Soseki Natsume and Ogai Mori.

Ohashi, Shintaro (1862-1944)
Industrialist and author.

Otori, Keisuke (1832-1911)
Military officer, lord, politician, Dutch language scholar, one time Principal of the Peers School (later Gakushuin University), he was Minister to China in 1889 and Envoy to Korea in 1893.

Oura, Kanetake
He was a politician, one time Minister of Communications and Chairman of the *Dai Nippon Butokukai*. Viscount Oura was suspected of corruption and retired from politics in 1915. Following his resignation, a decision was made by the *Dai Nippon Butokukai* to appoint military men rather than politicians to the post of chairman in the future.

Randori

Unlike kata, which is a series of prearranged techniques performed in slow motion, randori is a free practice bout in which any kind of judo throw or groundwork technique may be executed provided that it is performed in a safe manner.

Ritsu Sect

An ancient Buddhist school emphasizing ascetic discipline. One of the six sects of Nara Buddhism, it was introduced by Ganjin, a Chinese monk, who arrived in Japan in 754 AD.

Ryu

A style of jujutsu or other Japanese art usually named after the founder of the school. Jujutsu is divided into a great number of *ryu*. Some schools use swords, daggers, spears etc., whereas at other schools only unarmed techniques are taught. At the height of its popularity in the 17th century, there were reportedly over 700 schools teaching jujutsu. Though the names of the *ryu* were sometimes different, many were teaching the same or similar techniques. Once a student became a master, he would open a school under his own name, even though all the techniques that he taught to his students were perhaps no different from those that he had learned from his former master.

Saigo, Shiro (1866-1922)

A talented lightweight judo man trained by Kano. Saigo was an early celebrity, one of the four 'Guardians of the Kodokan', the others being Yoshitsugu Yamashita, Sakujiro Yokoyama and Tsunejiro Tomita. Saigo was famous for his throwing techniques, especially Yama-arashi. He was the inspiration for the famous book *Sugata Sanshiro* by Tsuneo Tomita, which was later turned into the popular 1943 motion picture *Sugata Sanshiro*. Written and directed by the famed Akira Kurosawa, *Sugata Sanshiro* is the story of a young man who struggles to learn the meaning of judo and in doing so learns something of the meaning of life. Saigo was posthumously awarded sixth dan by Kano, thus becoming the first ever to attain this grade.

Saigo, Tanomo (1830-1905)

A famous aikijujutsu master who adopted Shiro Saigo.

Saionji, Prince Kinmochi (1850-1940)

A statesman who took part in the Meiji Restoration, and later spent ten years in France. He served in several Cabinets under Ito and was president of the Privy Council (1900-1903). Prime Minister (1906-8, 1911-12), he escaped assassination in the military coup of February 1936.

Sake

A slightly sweet, colorless, noncarbonated wine made from rice.

Seiryoku Zenyo

This is one of Kano's two principal mottoes (the other being *Jita Kyoei*) that he stressed both in judo and in life. He regarded the training of the spirit as an important part of judo. Because of the variety of nuances it carries, it is not a simple matter to translate it into a pithy English expression. There are a number of ways that it may be translated. The usual rendition is: maximum efficiency or maximum efficient use of one's energy for worthy causes. The message that Kano was trying to convey seems to be that we should never waste our time or energy, but use them wisely by directing all efforts towards the successful outcome of some worthwhile cause.

Sen

Formerly a unit of Japanese currency, 100th part of one yen.

Shibusawa, Eiichi (1840-1931)

One time Minister of Finance, industrialist, trustee, auditor of the Kodokan and widely regarded as the father of modern Japanese business. His epiphany came at the age of 27 when he joined a Japanese delegation to the Paris Universal Exposition. This afforded him a firsthand look at the Western system of banking and industry. In 1873 he established Japan's first modern bank, the Daiichi Ginko. In the late 19th century, he became famed as a financier and was linked to more than 500 companies.

Shimoda, Utako (1854-1936)

Well-known educator, noted especially for her promotion of women's education. Founder of Jissen Women's College.

Shinagawa, Viscount Yajiro (1843-1900)

Studied in England and Germany in 1870. Leading politician, Cabinet Minister, one of the founders of the Kokumin Kyokai political party, instrumental in bringing about the Satsuma-Choshu alliance that preceded the Meiji Restoration in 1868.

Shinai

An imitation sword made of four tied strips of bamboo, with a hilt, often used in martial arts training, especially during kendo practice.

Shinken Shobu

A fight to the death, such as that fought with edged weapons on the field of battle. The spirited exertions of the antagonists in such an encounter are more intense and thus distinguish it from those usually exhibited in a mere sporting encounter.

Shinken Shobu no Kata

Both armed and unarmed kata techniques based on a life or death struggle.

Shochugeiko

Similar to the objectives of Kangeiko, which is held in mid-winter, Shochugeiko is a month-long series of twice daily hard judo training sessions held in mid-summer.

Smiles, Samuel (1812-1904)

The eldest of eleven children, born in Haddington, East Lothian, Scotland. Smiles became a well-known political reformer and moralist. He left school at the age of 14 and was apprenticed to a doctor, eventually enabling him to study medicine at Edinburgh University. He campaigned for parliamentary reform and contributed articles to the Edinburgh Weekly Chronicle. In May 1840 he was appointed secretary to the Leeds Parliamentary Reform Association, but after his support for Chartism waned, he began to form his theory of developing the self, which eventually found expression in his publications, especially so in his world-famous book, Self-Help (1859).

Sojutsu
The ancient art of fighting with spears.

Spencer, Herbert (1820-1903)
Philosopher, born in Derby, England. Prominent thinker of the Victorian age, despite early struggles, Spencer had by the 1870s become the most famous philosopher of the age. His works were translated into many languages including German, Italian, French, Russian, Spanish, Chinese and Japanese.

Sutemi Waza
The classification of judo throws in which the attacker sacrifices himself by purposely falling to the mat while in the process of throwing his opponent. Sutemi waza are divided into *masutemi* (supine sacrifice) and *yokosutemi* (side sacrifice) throws.

Suzuki, Masaya (1861-1922)
A former student of Kano, he graduated from Tokyo University in 1887. Businessman and leader of the giant Sumitomo combine. He joined Sumitomo after serving in the Home Ministry and the Agriculture and Commerce Ministry.

Tachiwaza
Judo techniques executed in the standing position. These are mainly throws, but occasionally include arm locks and strangulation techniques.

Takagi, Kanehiro (1849-1920)
Born in Miyazaki Prefecture, studied medicine in London from 1875-1880. He became a naval medical officer, and was especially noted for his successful treatment of patients suffering from beriberi. Founded a medical school and hospital in Tokyo.

Takezoe, Shinichiro (1842-1917)
Father of Sumako, wife of Jigoro Kano. Takezoe was a former diplomat, one time Japanese Minister to Korea, scholar of Chinese literature and later a lecturer at Tokyo University.

Tani, Taketa

Major General Taketa Tani was the famed last commander of Kumamoto Castle, Kyushu, where he led a force of 4,600 men. Although besieged and greatly outnumbered by Takamori Saigo's army of some 9,000 men at arms in the dying days of the Shogunate in 1877, he heroically resisted the superior forces until most of his men were slain and the castle eventually fell.

Tani, Tateki (1837-1911)

Army lieutenant general, viscount, one time Principal of Gakushuin, member of the House of Peers and Minister of Agriculture & Commerce in the first Ito Cabinet.

Tani, Yukio (1881-1950)

Legendry jujutsu super star, arrived in the U.K. in 1899 at the invitation of Barton Wright, a British engineer who became his manager. The diminutive Tani, 5ft. 6 ins. tall, for some ten years toured the music hall circuit issuing challenges for prize money to champion boxers and wrestlers of any weight. Renowned for his many successes, he reportedly amassed a fortune of some 250,000 pounds and later became chief judo instructor at the London Budokwai.

Tokyoku Senshuken Taikai

The modern Asian Games were inaugurated in 1951, but these international games have their roots in the Tokyoku Senshuken Taikai (Far East Championships), a competition primarily between China, Japan and the Philippines regularly held between 1913 and 1934.

Tomita, Tsunejiro (1865-1937)

Kano's first judo pupil, who together with Shiro Saigo became the first to be awarded black belt grade. One of the four 'Guardians of the Kodokan'. His son, Tsuneo Tomita, became a famous novelist.

Tomita, Tsuneo (1904-1967)

Popular novelist. Best known for his judo novels *Sugata Sanshiro* (1942) and *Yawara* (1964-1965).

Toso

A sweetened rice wine mixed with spices. Toso is customarily served during New Year celebrations.

Totsuka, Hikosuke (1813-1886)

Head of the well-known Yoshin Ryu Totsuka-ha jujutsu school. Totsuka taught at a dojo in Agata-cho, Tokyo, where he reportedly instructed over three thousand students.

Ume, Kenjiro (1860-1910)

Doctor of Laws, one time President of Hosei University, Tokyo.

Uzawa, Somei (1872-1955)

Doctor of Laws, politician, and formerly a President of Meiji University, Tokyo.

Wakatsuki, Reijiro (1866-1949)

Statesman. Minister of Finance 1912-1915. Prime Minister 1926-1927, 1931. In 1930 he was chief Japanese delegate to the London Naval Conference. From 1933 to 1936 he spoke out strongly against Japanese militarism.

Yamagata, Aritomo (1838-1922)

Political leader in the Meiji and Taisho periods. Prime Minister from 1889 to 1891 and again from 1898 to 1900. Army general, commander of the First Army, active in the Sino-Japanese War of 1894-1895, Chief of Staff during the Russo-Japanese War of 1904-1905. For the last twenty years of his life, he was reportedly Japan's most influential elder statesman.

Yamashita, Yoshitsugu (1865-1935)

One of the four 'Guardians of the Kodokan'. Both Yamashita and his wife taught judo in the U.S. in the early 1900s. President Theodore Roosevelt gained a 1st Kyu grade under his tutelage. Following his death in 1935, Yamashita was posthumously awarded the world's first ever 10th dan grade.

Yokosutemi waza

The classification of judo throws in which the thrower sacrifices himself by falling onto the mat on his left or right side during the process of throwing his opponent.

Yokoyama, Sakujiro (1869-1912)

Assisted Jigoro Kano in establishing the Kodokan. One of the four 'Guardians of the Kodokan', known for his great skill in *sutemiwaza* or sacrifice techniques. Yokoyama later became a judo instructor and a director of the Kodokan.

Yuasa, Takejiro

Naval lieutenant commander. One of the first judo men to receive 10th dan grade.

Yuko no Katsudo

Monthly magazine of some 160 pages published in 1921 & 1922 to which Jigoro Kano and other prominent scholars contributed a large number of essays.

Zoshikai

Society founded by Prof. Jigoro Kano in 1898 for the purpose of developing the character of the nation's youth. This society published the monthly magazine *Kokushi,* (patriot) which contained many contributions from Kano, Masujiro Honda, et al.

Zoshikan

Famous school founded in 1773 by the Satsuma clan for the education of boys of samurai. Later, administered by the Bakufu government which favored western learning in addition to traditional Japanese education. Name changed in 1901 to Number Seven High School, Zoshikan.

BIBLIOGRAPHY

Kano Jigoro Chosakushu (Collected Works of Jigoro Kano) Volume III (Japanese) (Tokyo, 1992, Gogatsu Shobo)

Jijoron (Japanese) translated version of *Self-Help* by Hitoshi Takeuchi (Tokyo, 2005 edition, Mikasa-shobo)

Jinsei wa furu kousu (Japanese) Biography of Nobuo Murakami by Yoh Sato (Tokyo, 1996, Tokyo Shoseki)

Self-Help by Samuel Smiles (London, 1958 edition, John Murray)

The Spirit of Budo by Trevor Pryce Leggett (Tokyo, 1993, The Simul Press Inc.)

Mind over Muscle (writings of Jigoro Kano, compiled by Naoki Murata) (Tokyo, 2005, Kodansha International)

The Dragon Mask by Trevor Pryce Leggett (London, Ippon Books Ltd.)

Kodokan New Japanese-English Dictionary of Judo (Tokyo, 2000, Kodokan)

INDEX

E

Economics 12, 30, 57, 116
Eishoji 13, 23-25, 31, 69, 83, 171, 176
ethics 67, 90
Europe 52, 53, 57, 106, 128, 160
European Judo Union 160, 166

F

Flower arrangement 176
France 25, 53, 154, 182
Fukuda, Hachinosuke xvi, 3, 173, 175
Fukushima, Kanekichi 4, 6, 7

G

Germany 47, 53, 130, 166, 173, 183
Godai, Ryusaku 5
Grant, Ulysses Simpson 5
Gymnastics 13, 66, 67, 70, 142

H

Hakama 32, 33, 174
Hida, Shosaku 2, 16,
Hirose, Takeo 48, 50, 174
Holland 129, 173
Honda, Masujiro 29, 33, 48, 53, 174, 176, 187
House of Peers 20, 111-113, 176, 185
Hungary 131

I

Iikubo, Tsunetoshi xvi, 11-13, 35, 37, 50, 174
Ikuei Gijuku 1, 2
Imai, Genshiro 2
Inspection tour 44, 53, 56
International Judo Federation 160
International Olympic Committee xviii, 129, 158
Iso, Masatomo xvi, 5, 9, 175
Italy 129, 165, 173

ISBN 142516349-1

9 781425 163495

SEP 2010

796.
8152
WAT

Watson, Brian.
  Judo memoirs of Jigoro
Kano

Amherst Library

DISCARD

AMHERST PUBLIC LIBRARY
221 SPRING STREET
AMHERST, OHIO 44001

6687926R0

Made in the USA
Lexington, KY
13 September 2010